GRATITUDE
IN MOTION

GRATITUDE
IN MOTION

A TRUE STORY OF HOPE, DETERMINATION, AND THE
EVERYDAY HEROES AROUND US

COLLEEN KELLY ALEXANDER
WITH JENNA GLATZER

CENTER
STREET

New York   Nashville

Center Street
Hachette Book Group
1290 Avenue of the Americas, New York, NY 10104
centerstreet.com
twitter.com/centerstreet

First Edition: January 2018

Center Street is a division of Hachette Book Group, Inc. The Center Street name and logo are trademarks of Hachette Book Group, Inc.

The publisher is not responsible for websites (or their content) that are not owned by the publisher.

The Hachette Speakers Bureau provides a wide range of authors for speaking events. To find out more, go to www.HachetteSpeakersBureau.com or call (866) 376-6591.

Library of Congress Cataloging-in-Publication Data has been applied for.

ISBNs: 978-1-4555-7113-0 (hardcover); 978-1-4555-7114-7 (ebook)

Printed in the United States of America

LSC-C

10   9   8   7   6   5   4   3   2

With great honor I dedicate this book to my brother Erin Kelly. Thank you for being my first hero. Thank you for helping me throughout my own conflicted adolescent journey and into adulthood. Thank you for always being there. Thank you for showing me what the unconditional love of Christ looks and feels like. Over the course of multiple relationships, failed marriages, horrible diagnoses, far too many surgeries, equally as many post-anesthesia phone calls, joys, moose sightings, selfies with the best beer, and tears on four a.m. calls, you always have my back. You are the truth teller. I may not have always liked what you have had to say, but you have always spoken with integrity and pure grit. You have helped mold me into the wife, advocate, survivor, and person I am in this crazy world. You are the anchor of our family, and I am forever blessed you are my friend.

GRATITUDE
IN MOTION

Contents

CONTENTS

Foreword

by Bart Yasso

COLLEEN'S STORY TOUCHED ME in a very personal way. I've been commuting to work by bicycle for the past thirty years and have ridden my bike across the United States twice. I understand the vulnerability of cruising along on a bicycle in the midst of speeding cars and distracted drivers—your life can change forever in a split second. What separates Colleen from the rest of us is what she did with her very unfortunate circumstances.

I met Colleen in 2014 at the Gasparilla Distance Classic in Tampa, Florida, when we were both invited to the event as motivational speakers. The night before the big race, we shared our stories to inspire others on their journeys to the finish line the next morning. I was spellbound by Colleen's presentation. I was ready to head out the door and start running the minute she finished her talk. It was because of the way she involved the entire audience and the way she made us all feel very grateful for what we have. Never could I have foreseen the friendship and bond we forged that night and how often our paths would cross.

Colleen's first and only marathon came in September 2014. She and her husband, Sean, stayed at my home the night before the big race. As fate would have it, she had picked a marathon in my hometown, Bethlehem, Pennsylvania, where the course is only a few miles from my house. When Colleen set off for the starting line of the Lehigh Valley Health Network Via Marathon, I'm assuming with some trepidation, I could see a damaged body, but I sensed that the love between her and Sean would outweigh her physical limitations. Running 26.2 miles is very arduous. Running 26.2 miles in Colleen's condition I can't fathom, and I've run many marathons. I was out on the course cheering on runners, waiting to see Colleen pass. I saw a runner coming down the road hugging everyone in sight—every volunteer, every spectator, and every course marshal— and, yes, of course, this runner turned out to be my dear friend Colleen. I shouted, "Stop hugging everyone! You'd better keep running; the clock is ticking." Colleen has her own clock—it doesn't judge someone by time but by joy. By the smile on her face and the joy she was radiating, based on the Colleen clock she was winning the race. She finished by running into Sean's arms, a warm embrace, a marathon run by one but celebrated by thousands. Their love for each other touched me in a profound way. Colleen's marathon had nothing to do with running; it was 26.2 miles of love, joy, and an acceptance of making the best of what you have.

What I love most about Colleen is that she always thanks everyone who played a role in her survival. She knows firsthand the love and commitment of our first responders and all the health care workers who helped her, all the way down to the generous people who donated blood to keep her alive. She feels a very strong connection with hundreds of people in this journey and she wants to thank them all.

When a race starts, we all follow the same path to the finish line, but we all take very different paths to make it to the starting line. Colleen's path is a journey of survival, gratitude, love, and a boatload of courage to overcome so many obstacles. Colleen has taught me so many life lessons. She literally is gratitude in motion.

Running is the ultimate faith healer, restoring belief not only in oneself but in life's possibilities.

Introduction

THERE ARE SOME THINGS you learn when you get run over by a freight truck.

It was a beautiful fall day and I had just opened up a great new chapter in my life: I was a thirty-six-year-old newlywed with a fulfilling job where I knew I was making a difference in kids' lives, and my husband and I were doing triathlons together and talking about starting a family. Things were finally going according to plan—and then the plan got set on fire, courtesy of an impatient driver who blew a stop sign.

But you learn.

Mostly, you learn how to be grateful for every tiny thing you probably took for granted before. You spend a lot of time lying down in hospital beds with nothing but your thoughts, and that can go one of two ways: You can drown in your own sorrow (which I did for some time), or you can realize that even with the pain, the permanent disfigurement, the nightmares, and the limitations, life is still not only worthwhile but beautiful.

Don't get me wrong: I would rather have learned that lesson without getting flattened on the street, but that's how it went.

All my life, I'd defined myself as an athlete—a cyclist, mostly, considering that my dad owned a bike shop and I'd practically grown up there learning about bike mechanics. I wasn't even four when I got on my first bike. In my twenties, I'd already had to deal with significant health challenges that affected my competitive abilities. But I could not have pictured the absolute derailment of my life that was to come, and I could not have imagined getting through it and smiling at the end of it all. In the thick of it, there were many days and nights when I wished I had just died on the road rather than endure the constant daily pain and humiliation of a body that could no longer function without machinery and tubes and bags.

What pulled me out of it were the heroes: more than two hundred people who had collaborated to save my life. So many people teamed up just so I could live to see another sunset, take another walk with my dog, plant another garden. The path back to an active life was fraught with difficulties and setbacks, some of which are permanent, but along the way I learned to keep my focus on gratitude and live my life accordingly—not only *feeling* thankful, but acting on my thankfulness. The more I found ways to give back, the better I felt.

Now I'm ready to share my journey in the hope that you will find value in it. We're all connected in this world, and it's our job to look out for one another. Just as many people have looked out for me, I hope I can now be a light for people who are seeking one. Thank you for reading my story.

Chapter 1

First Love

I FOLDED THE LOOSE-LEAF note meticulously into an origami triangle, the way high school kids in the nineties did. On the outside was his name: *Sean.* On the inside were the words that might just lead to young romance—or crushing heartbreak:

> *I've heard lots about you and I thought it would be cool to get to know you . . . if you want, you can call me tonight at eight.*

Would I actually have the nerve to give it to him? That remained to be seen.

Sean walked with his head permanently tilted to the right side because his wavy, sun-kissed brown surfer hair covered his eye otherwise. He was six foot four, with a deep voice and a permanent tan from the Daytona Beach sun. He was a senior and I was a sophomore. I thought he was hot.

He was my friend's older brother, and I hadn't paid much attention to him before mutual friends of ours started buzzing in both our ears about what a good match we'd make. So I started checking him out. Unobtrusively, of course. Before long, I was arriving at school early just to catch a glimpse of his car pulling into the parking lot. He drove a black 1972 Volkswagen Beetle with surf racks on the top and subwoofers in the back. He was so effortlessly cool and yet didn't seem to have any grasp of his effect on girls. There were plenty of us who hoped to catch his eye, but he was more focused on surfing than dating...or much of anything else. I could have gone gray and wrinkled waiting for him to make the first move. He was sweetly oblivious.

What I liked about him, too, was his innocence. Lots of high school guys—especially seniors—were all about partying and getting drunk and having sex in other people's bathrooms. Sean wasn't like that. There was a rumor that he'd lost his virginity but had decided not to have sex again after that...which was attractive to me because I had already committed not to have sex before I was married.

My parents were Southern Baptists, and church was a major part of my life. I was devoted to God mostly out of a fear of mortality—I didn't want to make Him mad and wind up in hell. And there were apparently lots of ways to wind up there, but one of the quickest ways was to have sex before marriage.

I wasn't really sure what Sean's religious beliefs were, but that was pretty far back in my mind at the moment. God wouldn't mind if we just maybe kissed a little, would He?

With that hope in mind, I felt my face go white-hot as I approached Sean with my note in hand, clutched against my chest. We'd never really spoken before, aside from quick hellos. I walked up with all the false confidence I could muster, smiled, and handed it to him. Then I walked away in my acid-washed jeans without saying a word.

Smooth.

My brother Erin and I had just gotten our own phone line, so I sat in my room that night and waited eagerly for its distinctive ring. For effect, I turned on my music much louder than it needed to be just before eight o'clock so that I'd sound cool when I picked up the phone. Living Colour's "Cult of Personality" would really camouflage the sound of girl-sitting-by-the-phone. Right on time, it rang. I waited two rings to pick it up because...you know.

"Hello?"

"Hi. Colleen?"

"Oh, yes. Let me just turn down my music."

And so it started. I want to tell you that we had deep talks about the meaning of life, but we really just talked about school and our teachers and the other things high school kids talk about. Then we made plans for our first date at Friendly's.

He picked me up in that Volkswagen Bug that I had admiringly stalked for months. The view from the passenger seat was a little different from what I expected, though...you could actually see the road if you looked down. The floor had rusted-out holes right through the metal.

Depeche Mode was blaring through the subwoofers, and the whole car smelled of Sean's Cool Water cologne. He rolled down the windows, which was a *disaster*. I had so much hairspray in my well-thought-out hairdo, and wind and hairspray are a terrible combination. My hair had not yet gotten the memo that we were out of the eighties, and it had two natural enemies: water and wind.

Once I was in Sean's car, I had no idea what to say, and apparently neither did he, because we drove along for a good ten to twelve minutes saying absolutely nothing.

Nothing.

I was dumbstruck by insecurities; there was a whole movie's worth of inner monologue happening in my mind as I desperately tried to look cool and unaffected by the wind—not terrified that I would emerge from this vehicle looking like Tammy Faye Bakker. Once a silence gets started, it's very hard to end it. Eventually, as we were crossing a bridge, Sean took the plunge.

"So...do you still want to go to Friendly's?"

"Yeah. Sure."

I smiled nervously. In a non-windblown way.

After we got there, we both eased into real live conversation. We ordered big, sloppy burgers and Cokes and talked about our mutual friends.

"I nicknamed you Colleeny-Bopper," he said. "Because of how you're always bopping down the halls with so much energy and a big smile on your face."

"Well, I don't have a nickname for you yet. But my friend calls you Lurch because you're so tall and have that deep voice."

Maybe it wasn't the most flattering nickname.

He complimented me on my big blue eyes, and there was some banter about his cool hair. I had butterflies the whole time we sat there, and nervous giggles filled the air. When we were done eating, we went to play putt-putt golf.

By the end of the night, not only did I know that Sean was going to be my boyfriend, but he already felt like my best friend, too. We had such a great, playful rapport, and he was so sweet to me. I didn't get the feeling that he was just waiting till the right moment to get me to "park" and rip off my clothes. In fact, he didn't even kiss me that night.

Sean was so respectful of not only me, but my parents, too. He never pushed my curfews or did anything that would cause them to worry. Our relationship was innocent and joyful, consisting of lots of lunch dates to Wendy's and Taco Bell, movies, and trips to the beach.

The first time we went to the beach together, I wore a tankini, but it wasn't the shape of my body that I was nervous about...it was my feet. I buried my toes in the sand as quickly as possible after taking my shoes off, and hoped he wouldn't notice if I kept them buried, like an ostrich avoiding a predator. But he noticed.

"Why are you hiding your feet?"

"My toes," I said. "They're ugly."

"Come on, let me see."

"Nope."

"Do you see these things?" He pointed at his own—okay, yes, odd—toes. "These are called hammertoes. It can't be worse than that."

"Yes, it can. My friends always make fun of me. My feet are too big in general, but my second toes are really long."

"Well, now you have to show me."

Peer pressure.

I showed him. And he didn't make fun of me. Yet.

"There's nothing wrong with your feet! Those are the coolest toes I've ever seen!"

We did get to a point where we gleefully made fun of each other's quirks and flaws, but he was so good about being sensitive and building me up so that I'd always feel safe with him. It was a wonderful feeling. It was also ridiculous that he liked my giant toes.

Surfing was a huge part of his life, and he tried to teach me, but I was terrified. A few times, I paddled out with him and sat on a surfboard, but only once did I manage to stand upright. The rest of the time I mostly spent fantasizing about when I would be allowed to paddle back to shore. I didn't like the feeling of not being able to see land, or of waiting for a wave and hoping I'd get my balance right in time.

So after that, I would just sit on the beach and watch him, and then we'd go out for greasy food afterward. I was a serious athlete, primarily a cyclist, but I could still down cheese fries with the best of them.

Every Sunday, I went to church with my family, and Sean came with us a few times. Sometimes he also went to church with his parents. They were Episcopalian, which was much different from being Baptist. Episcopalians were barely Christians at all, in my pastor's mind. It was a much more liberal religion.

When Sean once again didn't go to church one Sunday, I asked him why.

"The ocean is my church," he said. "When I want to be spiritual and connect, that's where I go."

I sort of understood. But I sort of didn't.

He asked me to prom, which was a big deal for a sophomore. I borrowed a black dress I'd admired from my oldest brother Shawn's wife, Kaori, and my dad told us to be back by eleven. It wasn't much time on a prom night, but we knew he meant business. Whenever my curfew neared, my dad would wait near the door and flick the lights on as we approached to let us know he was watching.

Sean and I took pictures at his parents' house and then in a garden where we had often taken walks before, then headed to the Daytona Beach Desert Inn with friends and danced for hours. It marked the end of his high school years; I still had two more to go, and I wondered how that would affect us. Lots of couples broke up when someone went to college, but it didn't seem like we would.

The night before my birthday that August, Sean plotted a surprise for me with my parents: He sneaked in after I fell asleep and put a vase of flowers and teddy bear wearing a cameo necklace in my bathroom, along with a tape player hooked up to the outlet. It was rigged so that the play button was already pressed, but the power wouldn't turn on until someone (me, hopefully) turned on the light. When I did, it played our song: "I'll Be There" by Escape Club. He'd bought a single of the cassette.

It was the most romantic thing anyone had ever done for me, and I was amazed that my parents let him do it. I still have the cassette.

Sean wasn't exactly my first boyfriend; I'd been out on dates with lots of guys before, but this was the first relationship that lasted more than a couple of weeks. It was exciting to me, filled with all the heady feelings of first love. We had never actually used that word, but I had thought it plenty.

My youth minister and his wife noticed how head-over-heels I seemed to be, and when they asked how the relationship was going, I even confided that I felt like I might be falling in love. It wasn't received the way I thought it would be.

"Do you know if he's saved?" my youth minister asked.

"I don't know," I said. "Maybe. He goes to church sometimes."

"Have you witnessed to him yet?"

I looked down.

"Colleen, if you haven't, you need to. If he's not saved, then you have the responsibility to tell him about Jesus. Otherwise he could go to hell."

"I just try to live my life as a Christian and be a good example."

"But that's not enough. This relationship can't work right now because you're unequally yoked. Paul tells us in 2 Corinthians 6:14, 'Be ye not unequally yoked together with unbelievers: for what fellowship hath righteousness with unrighteousness? And what communion hath light with darkness?' You have nothing in common with Sean. If you're choosing to be yoked with someone who isn't saved, then you're in sin."

I stood there listening, a knot forming in my stomach. What was he telling me? My relationship with Sean was sinful?

"You have to put God first in your life," he said.

It was a small town; the youth minister knew that Sean's family wasn't very religious. And although every word he said to me hurt, I felt that he was looking out for me as he always had. He and his wife had become a big part of my life and my thoughts during my adolescence; he looked for ways for all of us in the youth group to deepen our relationship with God and be better Christians. He wasn't telling me this because he wanted to ruin my life—it was because he cared about me and didn't want to see me make a big mistake. Their convictions were strong.

It was just so different from the way I thought, though. I told him I'd pray and think about it, and then as soon as I got home, I couldn't stop crying. Had I been letting Sean down all this time by not proselytizing to him? I had never been comfortable with evangelism, but was I being a terrible friend by not helping to save his soul? What if the minister was right and I was throwing away the only opportunity to help Sean get into heaven?

I'd told the minister I didn't know whether Sean was saved, but deep down I knew he wasn't saved like I was in the Baptist Church. I'd just never asked because I didn't want to hear the answer. While he supported me as a Christian, religion wasn't a big part of his life, and I couldn't imagine telling him that he needed to devote his life to Jesus if he wanted to continue dating me.

All that night, I prayed and cried, cried and prayed. It was torture. I knew that I was going to have to break up with Sean to prove my devotion to God, but it made such little sense to me. Our relationship had been so pure, not lustful. How could it be sinful to fall in love?

When I finally emerged from my room, my parents were waiting on the living room couch to talk to me.

"I think I have to break up with Sean," I told them. "I don't think he's saved."

The tears wouldn't stop streaming, and my parents were very supportive.

"We're proud of you for taking a stand for Jesus," my dad said. My mom gave me a hug and told me I was doing the right thing. I hoped she was right.

The next time Sean came over, I met him at the door and fell into his arms crying.

"What's wrong?" he asked.

"We have to break up," I managed to get out in between sobs.

"Why?"

I couldn't answer. Nothing I said would make sense. I tried and tried to say something—anything—to give him an explanation, but I just couldn't get any words out.

"Are you sure this is what you want? Because you're crying right now . . ." he said.

I just nodded. He was so confused—but then, so was I. After several minutes, he let go of our embrace and left, and I was empty. He left there assuming that I was breaking up with him because he was going to college and I was still in high school. I didn't say, "Let's stay friends," because it would just be too painful to see him anymore if I couldn't be with him. I didn't think I would ever stop crying.

"Do you feel better?" my mother asked the next day.

"No," I said. "Everything hurts." My mom hugged me.

It continued to hurt like that for weeks. My friends, who had understood and accepted my other Christian "quirks" before, thought I was crazy for breaking up with him. It was the hardest thing I'd ever done, but I had to be right with my God. I had to trust in His plan for my life.

The new school year started and I never saw Sean's Volkswagen Beetle pull into that parking lot again. We'd never ditch the cafeteria or see *Robin Hood: Prince of Thieves* or walk through that beautiful garden again. I'd never stand on a higher step to kiss him so I could reach his lips. It was over.

And I really wasn't okay.

Chapter 2

Someone Else's Life

Even though Sean stayed local for college, I never ran into him. But my brother Erin did on their Daytona Beach college campus. Erin would come home and say, "Sean asked about you," and it was bittersweet—nice to know he cared, but still painful. It felt like we were star-crossed.

Erin and I were close and he knew my reasons for ending the relationship. I think he was as confused as I was about the whole thing—we both understood that this was what I was supposed to do, but it didn't feel right to either of us.

I trusted my brother deeply; he had saved my life when my inner tube flipped over and I nearly drowned in a pool at age five. I still remember looking up and seeing his shadowy, skinny body over me as I choked and spluttered out all the chlorinated water from my lungs.

He had been my first hero. I didn't know then that there would be others.

That fall, I tried to go about my normal life and move on. It was a busy year of exploration—I was heavily involved with sports and activities: choir, band, marching corps, flag corps, debate club, Fellowship of Christian Athletes (I was the vice president), Thespian Society, along with my church and youth group. Basically, if there was a club around that didn't involve doing math or playing *Dungeons & Dragons*, I was in it.

My senior year was not particularly memorable except that I met Jesse, a missionary boy whom my parents and youth leaders instantly approved of. He was three years older than I was and was beginning a career as a pilot. He asked to take me to my prom and I thought he must be the one. All the ducks were in a row: He was a Christian who was going to have a good career, I thought he was attractive, we both agreed on no premarital sex, all the important adults in my life gave their approval...I was not wildly in love with him, but maybe that didn't matter. It was supposed to be God's plan, not mine.

When Jesse proposed to me, I was nineteen years old and had just finished my first year at community college. Part of me was mad because now I had to say yes. It took away the possibility of feeling anything stronger for anyone. But I told myself that I was ready. Lots of other young women in my church married young and were starting families. It was *not* normal among my non-church friends, who thought I was crazy. They came to my wedding wearing pained expressions, sitting in the pews singing along to church hymns while hung over from partying at college.

My gown was a huge, ornate thing with sequins and pearls and a long train. Our wedding planner was a young woman from church who had also gotten married at nineteen. She helped me pick out my all-silk flowers and candles and hunter-green velvet ball gowns for my eight bridesmaids.

Alcohol and dancing were both frowned upon at weddings according to the church, so we didn't have either of those. We did have a harpist, and my parents and the church elders made all the food for the reception. It was very churchy and kind of boring.

Then came the wedding night.

I was terrified about getting pregnant, and our first experience together was painful.

I have to do this again? I fretted after it was over.

Reality set in quickly after the wedding. In order for Jesse to fly commercially, he had to log a lot more hours in flight, and he had to pay for those hours of training. I dropped out of school and worked two, sometimes three, jobs at a time to support us. I didn't even think about finishing my college degree or chasing some kind of dream job because I understood my role was to support my husband. Anything else would be selfish.

I knew what the path would be—it was laid out clearly. I would work until his career was solid, then I'd get pregnant and stop working and my life would be about raising kids. That's how it was for almost all my church friends who were a little older than me. They baked casseroles at five p.m. and had tea sets for their kids and middle-class houses in middle-class neighborhoods. It was all very simple and normal, and I had found some comfort in the idea before.

I took business classes and a certified nursing assistant program at the local community college and then began working as a nurse's aide full-time, often picking up double shifts. It was exhausting, but it was a job. During off hours, I'd do filing for a couple of doctors or work with the children's programs at church. It was a lot of obligations, but it was fine. Wasn't it fine?

Maybe it wasn't.

A year and a half into the marriage, we moved to Vermont, where Jesse was on salary with TWA. He was often working abroad and I could no longer ignore what was happening in my heart. Things were falling into place just the way they were supposed to, and yet when I took stock of my life I panicked.

I did not really love this man; I don't think I ever had. Not the way I had loved Sean. Thinking about life apart from him didn't make me cry—it made me feel relief. I was watching my non-church friends living it up at college, and here I was throwing away any dreams I might have had for my own life so I could have kids with a man I didn't really love. It made me feel resentful, and the thought of bringing children into this barren ground pushed me over the edge.

I have to put an end to this, I thought. *This can't be where I'm supposed to be.*

I left and moved in with a few friends in Burlington, though Jesse cried and begged for me to stay. He would call and check to see if I'd changed my mind, and reminded me that God's will was for us to stay together. He alternated between upset and angry, and filled me with guilt. I agreed to give our marriage another try, but I was still deeply unhappy and finally took the chicken's way out: I waited until he had left for work in St. Louis and filed for divorce. I knew he would be gone for a week or so, and I hadn't alluded to any problems before he left. If I had told the truth, he wouldn't have gone and there would have been a big emotional struggle and I might have given in again.

I had him served with papers in St. Louis, which I know shocked him. My parents were concerned and upset.

"You're in sin. You're not following His will," my mother said.

"I can't stay in a marriage where I'm this unhappy. Don't you understand? All sins are equal in God's eyes, right? So if I ask for forgiveness and try to live a good life…"

"If you're looking for our blessing on this, we can't give it."

It was a dark time, but I didn't go back on my decision. Jesse wouldn't file because he felt it was a sin, so it was up to me to see it through. I didn't have the money for an attorney, so I didn't use one, but he did. There wasn't much to fight over, in my mind—I wasn't asking for support; I just wanted a clean break. But there was one thing he wanted to put in writing: He had his attorney indicate that I was having an affair. I wasn't. But apparently that would absolve him of the sin of divorce.

Once I had broken through that barrier of committing what my parents thought was a really huge sin, I felt I had little to lose, and I started making up for lost time.

It gave me the space to figure out who I was as an individual. For the first time, I stood on my own two feet and stared off into this vast unknown, knowing that no one else could live my life for me or tell me how I should live it. For too long, I'd been obeying rules that were not sitting right in my heart, and now I had to choose my own path, even if it meant alienating my family and some of my friends.

The loss of almost everything familiar made it feel like there was a big hole inside me, and I had to fill it up. I started working in human resources in the banking industry, and I began putting myself through community college again, taking classes in psychology and religion. I wanted to learn about religions aside from my own and what their belief systems entailed, not just what everyone had *told* me they were about. I partied with friends and drank too much, dated... I probably went overboard on just about everything. The more I tried to fill that empty space, the more untethered I felt.

One of the things that I counted on for some kind of grounding was cycling. Every day I felt the rhythmic motion of the pedals under my feet, a sort of meditation on wheels. And every day I also ran. Getting outdoors and being active was the best way to quiet my mind.

My parents were so upset that I was "secularized" and thought I would lose my faith in Christ, when in actuality, the opposite happened. It took a while of exploring to get there, though.

I started seeing all the aspects of my life as choices rather than obligations. I used to go to church on Sundays because that's just what you did; now I continued searching for a relationship with God that was something more personal and connected. I searched for communion with God in everyday places, and it felt empowering. Sin was no longer a black-and-white thing for me. Sometimes in life, we make errors, and through those errors, we find growth that can make us stronger. Not everything was a sin, I realized. Some things were just mistakes.

I went through therapy to help me try to figure things out—to unpack my whole past and try to determine what was real and true and what I could safely discard from my life. Then one day I decided to show up at a Quaker meeting, without knowing what to expect. There were about sixty people in the room, all shaking hands and greeting one another. It was a more diverse group than I'd imagined—all ages, some with tattoos, just "regular people" you'd see around town. After a few minutes, someone rang a bell and said it was time for the meeting.

We all sat in a big, open circle and each person offered a blessing to the person next to them, one at a time. Then, for the next fifteen minutes, it was mostly silent. You're supposed to just sit there and reflect and pray silently and speak only if you feel moved to do so by God.

This is so weird, I thought at first. I was uncomfortable without a priest speaking at the front of an altar, and I didn't know what to do with myself. But as I settled in, other feelings bubbled to the surface: I felt an energy of love and peace and equality.

After those fifteen minutes had passed, someone stood up and said, "I want to thank God because something wonderful has happened in my life. I thank God for this healing and light."

He spoke briefly about the blessing that had come into his life. That connected organically with another person in the room, who also stood and said thanks to God for a good resolution to a health problem, and another stood to say thanks for his family all spending the holidays together. Several others stood and shared, and all of them had a communal tie—like a brightly glowing light of interconnectedness. At the end, someone rang a bell and everyone shook hands or hugged, then we went off to share a meal together. They had a Bible study afterward.

It was powerful for me, anchoring me to the idea that God was in that space and with these people, not only in the particular type of church of my youth. It was enough to open my communication with God again. Even though I went just a few times, it was a beautiful experience that brought me into a community of strangers who didn't feel like strangers.

My parents were upset for quite a while about my divorce, but that improved with time as well. There was never any big, formal scene where we hugged it out, but they stopped bringing it up all the time and our conversations became less strained.

What I learned over this time was that while most of our families love us and want the best for us, they may not always know what is best for us. We need to take responsibility for our own lives and choices, even if it means disagreement and inciting anger. You can't let fear of what others will think or their disapproval keep you from being happy in your own life.

I was still in the midst of my exploration when something happened that changed my whole perspective: September 11.

Chapter 3

The Youth Center

THE TERRORIST ATTACKS OF September 11, 2001, changed the country and the world in irrevocable ways—and on a more microcosmic scale, rocked my life.

I was still living in Vermont then, and for months I'd been having vivid dreams that felt very real. In the early morning hours that day, I dreamed that I was covered in rubble and couldn't breathe. I awoke in a panic and it took me a while to get myself going.

It was just a dream, I told myself. *Get on with your day.*

But I couldn't shake it. Even as I made myself coffee, I looked down at my hands and felt like I saw the gray dust of the rubble, almost an out-of-body experience. I turned on the television and a plane had already hit the first tower.

And I had to go to work.

People were dying, I felt like I'd had a vision of it in my sleep and couldn't do anything to prevent it, and somehow I was supposed to clock in like it was any other day. I walked to work at the credit union, as usual, and I sat down at my desk and turned on the computer, trying to pretend that this could be anything like a normal workday. The banking industry had to go on. Conference calls and meetings were still happening. People were still calling about getting loans. Suddenly everything felt so trivial, and I began crying.

"I need to go home," I told my supervisor.

It was a morning when the whole world learned how fragile human life could be. The dating and drinking and period of discovery that had felt like my right felt so stupid now. I was watching the first responders on the news and feeling so personally helpless. The hatred that had driven these images tore me apart. What was I doing to combat any of this? How was my life serving any greater good? Working in human resources for corporate America was not improving the world.

Over the next few weeks I had a real paradigm shift. There was no time in this world for living a comfortable life, I decided. Getting through it day to day was not enough. I was working my way up in human resources and making a pretty good living, but it was time to figure out something more meaningful.

The man I was dating at the time, Paul, was an adjunct professor at the University of Vermont, and he knew of an organization active on campus that might be right for me: AmeriCorps.

It's like a domestic version of the Peace Corps. AmeriCorps is a nonprofit organization aimed at improving American communities, providing support and funding to programs in a variety of areas, including health, education, economic development, job training, public safety, and the environment. I reviewed their website and filled out an application to work with youth in need.

You can sign up for one or two years of service, and the organization will cover your basic needs, providing a living stipend that's right at the poverty level and health care, along with any training and certifications you need. Plus, it offers a good education stipend—$10,000 per year—which was attractive to me because I had higher hopes than community college. I could also apply for matching grants to double that figure. And because AmeriCorps offered only a living stipend, not an income, I also qualified for about $200 worth of food stamps per month; the instructions for applying were right in the AmeriCorps application.

The director of the state's substance abuse prevention group within AmeriCorps reviewed my résumé.

"This would be a step down for you in terms of where you are in your career."

"That's not something that worries me. I'm ecstatic to be here."

"What population do you hope to serve?" she asked.

"Teenagers," I answered. "I feel like support is so crucial during that time period."

I thought about all I had learned in therapy and how much I wanted to help pass along my newfound understanding to other kids who might have been struggling with their identities, family acceptance, or other issues. My life had been so narrow until then, without much diversity or understanding of other backgrounds. I liked the idea of not only opening myself up to meet different kinds of people, but helping facilitate that in others, too.

Teenage years can be so self-centered—and I don't mean that as an insult. It's just that those years are so much about self-discovery and independence that teens can become very myopic. What I hoped to instill in kids was the idea that part of our self-esteem, part of what is best about us, is found in what we do in service of others.

They found me the perfect position. Through AmeriCorps, in 2002 I began volunteering at a youth center in St. Albans, Vermont, that we soon renamed Common Ground. The center didn't have much going on—it was open only a couple of days a week and was deeply in debt, with no paid staff, only volunteers. It was in desperate need of funding and programs. That's where I came in; I signed on for a two-year term to write grant applications and find programs to help combat community problems like substance abuse and teen pregnancy. I didn't have much context for substance abuse, but I got significant training through the program.

In addition, I was also able to take more training through the Red Cross so that I was certified to teach CPR, HIV/AIDS education, babysitting safety training, lifeguarding, and more. I took whatever courses interested me and felt relevant, and even became a volunteer EMT on the weekends.

Soon after I was hired, we began opening the center three days a week, but it wasn't all that busy. Finally some of the kids opened up to me about the fact that the center had been known as a place for dorky kids and misfits, and maybe it would take some time to attract more of a crowd. I increased my efforts to make it "cool," making sure we were offering a variety of activities aimed at the jocks, the hippies, the nerds, and everyone in between. And the kids responded. They started showing up one by one and in groups, peeking in tentatively for the first time and deciding to stick around. This was going to be a safe haven for so many of them, and they didn't even know it yet.

Before long we were busy enough to open five days a week— plus take the kids on weekend trips. My job was multifaceted and included searching for funding, mentoring kids, running programs for them, managing volunteers, public speaking, traveling with our kids, tutoring (everything but math!)...within just a few months, there was so much going on there, and I helped to build it all.

It was an exciting time, made even more so by the fact that Paul proposed and we got married after we'd been dating for two years. I was afraid to take that leap, but also captivated by his free spirit. We came from very different backgrounds—his family was loud and liberal and Jewish, very loving and also very educated. They all lived nearby. Paul and I had a lot in common, like our love for dogs and our concern for the environment, but we also clashed sometimes over things like spirituality and the idea of wanting kids. He didn't want any, and I didn't think I did, either...at first. But that changed for me with time, and I hoped it would change for him, too.

One of the nicest parts of our relationship was that Paul often helped at the youth center. We had lots of regulars who showed up after school. Many of them started coming around really just because they didn't have anywhere else to go until their parents got home from work.

Several took leadership training so that they could volunteer at the center assisting other kids. They helped with greeting new people, making sure everyone signed in, cleaning the facility, researching programs and grants, everything. Lots of them came from difficult backgrounds, but we worked on choosing positive mind-sets in the face of adversity. When you realize that you don't always have control over your circumstances, but you do have control over your outlook, it can be empowering. We could always look for hope together.

What struck me was that our differences didn't make us so different after all. Teenagers are teenagers. The circumstances and the outsides might not look alike, but at heart, we were so much more a part of one another than not. We wanted love, respect, something to belong to, something to feel proud of, something that felt our own.

These kids' lives were often chaotic, and I imagined myself as a tree, planting myself deep in their lives, providing the reliable support and roots that they needed. It was such an honor to be accepted that way. I was not much older than some of them, but it was a parental role, and I deeply loved and appreciated it. For the first time, I felt like my life had real meaning and that I was fulfilling the role I was meant to play.

We depended on grant money to run the center. Our state senator Bernie Sanders was passionate about youth and helping to lift people in lower socioeconomic brackets, so he was wonderful to work with and gladly took meetings with me to discuss how the state could help boost our efforts.

"I have federal earmark money for community improvement left over. Write me a proposal," he said at one of our first meetings.

After writing up a strong plan and explanation of our services and gathering tons of letters of recommendation, we got three years of funding based on that conversation.

We started an organic garden so there would always be healthy food for the kids—they'd often go outside and dig up potatoes and bring them in so I could cook them and top them with some sour cream or cheese donated by Cabot Creamery. We had a lot of in-kind donations like that.

Over the summer we started a hiking club, and the kids formed a basketball program open to schools in the surrounding area. The music program was our most popular, though. We'd have alternative music nights once a week, and open up the space for band practice twice a week.

We built a stage and got amps and a couple of donated guitars, bongo drums, and microphones. It was a great place where kids could jam without getting yelled at for being too loud or not sounding good enough. (Vermont has some pretty cool neighbors, and we tried to keep the ending times respectful.) They'd have outdoor concerts in the summer, staged on a flatbed truck borrowed from a farmer, hard-core rocking out in the middle of a field with a generator in tow.

And the kids themselves…oh, the kids! I loved them all. I didn't know that I would as much as I did. They all had stories, and if you didn't respect how hard so many of them were working just to be okay, just to get through every day and be as amazing and positive as they were, you really weren't paying attention. They were the next group of heroes in my life.

Gail was one who particularly stood out. From a young age, she was around adults with drug, alcohol, and gambling addictions. Gail didn't know her own father and she had inconsistent father figures—the only steady male figure in her life was an uncle. The family also struggled financially; even with welfare and state assistance, she and her siblings never seemed to have the basics, and she had to help raise her baby sister.

She lived about two blocks away from the Common Ground building and heard all the hubbub about a new youth center, so she walked in one day when she was twelve.

Initially she was quiet, but once Paul and I were able to show her we weren't leaving and that we cared greatly for her, she bloomed. She participated in almost all of our activities, our youth council, and any outreach where I needed her. She became my little sister.

Paul and I had about two acres of land that we tilled and used to grow organic produce—primarily as a hobby, but also to sell at farmers' markets and area restaurants. We found work for Gail to do on our farm for a little money, and some days she'd sleep over at our house. Paul and I even discussed trying to adopt her, though we knew her mother would not give up parental rights.

Once she called in a heap of tears in the middle of the night. Even though I couldn't make out what she was saying, obviously something was devastatingly wrong. After a few moments she was able to get out that her uncle had attempted suicide earlier that day. Her family was a mess.

Just by chance, she had been riding in a car past her uncle's house and saw that there were police, fire trucks, and an ambulance outside his home. She told me how she'd watched Fireman Joe (a well-known local fire prevention officer and EMT) perform CPR on her uncle before the ambulance crew brought him to the hospital. They'd gotten a pulse back, but he was not conscious. Gail was devastated as she waited for news. A couple of days later, her uncle was disconnected from the ventilators, and the funeral was held shortly after.

Looking back, this was the most critical point in Gail's life. It solidified her decision not to go down the path that her family had followed.

"I want to be a paramedic and firefighter like Fireman Joe," she told me.

"I believe in you completely," I told her. "Just tell us how we can support you."

We knew she would not have family to bring her to college tours, or to help her fill out hours of paperwork and apply for financial aid. The Vermont Student Assistance Corporation came through for her, enabling her to be the first person in her family to go to college.

She was accepted at the only program she wanted to attend: Southern Maine Community College's fire science program. Paul and I were ecstatic. Her mother said nothing.

"You're going to do great things. Just stay true to yourself and go after your goals, and you'll get there," I said.

I cannot imagine the fortitude it took for this young woman to choose to walk away and create an entirely different life from the one she was expected to fall into. It was hard to say goodbye, but she kept in close touch, letting me know how well school was going and how she felt like all the students there were becoming a family.

Paul's cousin Jason was another amazing person who came into my life at this time. A filmmaker in South Africa who had worked with famous visionaries, he had done a lot of peace activism, and I was thrilled when he visited us for a week. We got into a conversation about the nonprofit he was working with in South Africa called PeaceJam, through which he had come to know the Dalai Lama and Archbishop Desmond Tutu.

PeaceJam's slogan is "Nobel Peace Laureates Mentoring Youth to Change the World." The whole idea was to educate kids about the world's best peace leaders, and encourage them to then use their knowledge to expand their cultural horizons, become more compassionate, and improve their communities. At the culmination of the program, the kids would go to a conference to actually meet and interact with one of the thirteen Nobel Peace Prize laureates who were involved with the organization—possibly from nearby, possibly from the other side of the world. It was a curriculum implemented in some schools and community programs, covering elementary through college students.

"That sounds so meaningful. What a great way to get kids to think about the world outside their town and become more empathetic," I said.

"You know, it's in the U.S., too. I wonder if there are any programs in Vermont," he said.

We checked online, but the closest one was in Massachusetts.

One of Jason's projects was a short film. He had written a line of music with his partner and then filmed people all over the world playing it with whatever instruments they wanted, in whatever style they wanted. Then he edited the video to blend all of them together, a showcase of different cultures uniting.

"Can I show it at your teen center one night and have a discussion about it?" he asked me.

"Uh...*yeah!*"

The kids were fascinated with him—this big Jewish hippie guy with a South African accent made quite an impression. They asked him all kinds of questions and he told them about PeaceJam.

"They have a website where you can sign up to start a program," he said, and as soon as the words came out of his mouth, I knew I was in trouble.

The kids looked at me with big eyes.

"Please? Pleeease, Colleen? Can we start it here?"

"We already have a lot of programs here. I'm in over my head writing grant applications…" I started, but it was a hard thing to fight against. I mean, how do you resist kids giving you doe eyes about learning peace?

"The only way I'll agree to this is if you guys train with me and we launch this together."

They were over the moon.

I went to a PeaceJam conference in Massachusetts to start the process of facilitator training. The first conference I attended with the kids was at a local college with Jody Williams, honored in 1997 for her work on the International Campaign to Ban Landmines. It was hardly her only civil activism work, though—she had been tirelessly campaigning for human rights since the Vietnam War.

The kids were so impressed with her, and what was even better was that she was from a small town in Vermont. There's something wonderful about seeing greatness and finding it accessible. This woman was from right here. She was not born a celebrity and bore no special markings on her forehead destining her for a life of importance. She was someone who had gone to a school like theirs and had friends like theirs and decided to make her life matter.

The funny thing, too, is that she wasn't what you might expect from a perpetual do-gooder—she wasn't prim or proper, she wasn't a "Kumbaya" person; she was passionate and angry and she sometimes used swear words. The kids, of course, thought that was *outstanding*.

One of them turned to me in astonishment and said, "She's a totally normal person."

I smiled. "Just like you and me."

"She's *amazing!*"

It reminded me of the misconceptions people have about peace activists. Advocating for nonviolence doesn't mean that we're flighty people who just want to carry around sunflowers all day and pretend the world is perfect. This kind of work doesn't mean one isn't angry. You can be angry—very angry—and still want to solve problems without weapons and warfare. In fact, there are so many things in this society that we *should* be angry about. As I like to say, peace is not for the weak.

There were about four hundred kids and fifty mentors at the conference, and Jody did a great job of getting them fired up. We talked about things that were going on right here in our community and then things that were going on in faraway places like Sudan that the kids had probably never thought much about. How could we draw parallels? How could we find root causes to work on to create sustainable change? It was so powerful.

They didn't know it then, but many of those kids ended up making lifelong friends at the conference. They traded contact information and stayed in touch, creating this web of caring kids growing into caring adults together.

I learned from Jody that when you're doing something that matters, *you* matter. Working with teens is what spoke to me, but it can be true of any cause that's important to your life. Everyone needs money to live, but more than that, we also need meaning to live, so it's important to find ways to spend significant time doing things that make us feel like we're making a difference for others. A full wallet can't fix an empty soul.

Our program in Vermont took off big-time. Soon there were programs at local high schools that attracted more than a hundred kids at a time. It was a resounding success, and so gratifying to have started it. In fact, everything in my life was looking pretty terrific.

And then the next tornado ripped through my world.

Chapter 4

Brain Surgery

Since my teen years, I'd had bad migraines. In my midtwenties, though, they got worse. I'd have to be in bed for a day or two with nausea and horrific pain like someone was stabbing me in the back of the head with a knife.

Doctors prescribed medications that didn't work, and when I went back again and again to ask if there was anything else we could do, one of them said that it was probably anxiety and depression that were triggering the migraines.

"Do you want to try Valium or a similar antianxiety medication?" he asked.

"I'll try anything. Right now I'm fantasizing about driving a nail into the back of my head to release the pressure."

The antianxiety medications didn't work, either. I was frustrated with the medical dead ends, and in 2007, I decided to try a chiropractor. He had a tough time adjusting the vertebrae in my neck, though, and said, "I think you're just too guarded—you're not letting yourself relax."

It's very hard to *try* to relax, but I did keep trying. I went back several times. Finally, after a few weeks, the chiropractor was able to make the adjustment he was trying to make to my neck, and he seemed pleased. However, within twenty-four hours, I was a total mess with a set of symptoms that terrified and baffled me.

The first time I went to the bathroom, I passed out on the toilet. For weeks afterward, anything that caused heightened body responses made me dizzy or caused me to actually lose consciousness. It happened if I raised my voice too loudly. It happened during sex (*such* a mood killer). It happened if I bent down to pick up something off a low shelf in the grocery store. I couldn't see straight. I was a wreck whenever I did anything that involved physical strain.

I had to stop volunteering as an EMT because I was more likely to *be* a patient than be capable of treating a patient.

Finally an MRI revealed a small cyst in the center of my brain, but the doctor said it was insignificant and probably not contributing to anything—just that it needed to be monitored to make sure it didn't grow or change. We did two repeat MRIs, but they found nothing else abnormal to explain my symptoms.

Within two or three months, I deteriorated further. The next troubling symptom was mixed-up word association.

"Can you hand me the pen?" I'd ask—when I didn't mean *pen*. I meant *phone*. And then I was totally confused when a friend handed me a pen, because clearly, hadn't I just said that I needed the phone?

Then there was the extreme forgetfulness. I'd put cauliflower in my grocery cart, then walk down the aisle and ten seconds later think, *I should get some cauliflower,* turn around and pick it up again—completely unaware that I had literally *just* put some in my cart.

Finally, I went to Dartmouth-Hitchcock Medical Center in New Hampshire to get another opinion. Doctors there did another MRI with contrast, and this time the results were very different: Within hours, I got a phone call saying that they thought they knew what was causing all my problems and that it was something fixable.

"You have an Arnold-Chiari malformation," my doctor told me. "They're relatively rare, but we set up a consultation with a neurosurgeon here for you next week."

As if I were going to just sit on my hands and wait that long. Of course, I began doing my own research and figured out the crux of what it meant: It was a structural defect in my cerebellum, which controls balance. Normally the cerebellum sits above the opening to the spinal canal, but with this kind of malformation, it protrudes below the spinal canal's opening. This puts pressure on the brain and can block the flow of cerebrospinal fluid. It's something that can form later in life due to injury or infection, but it's most commonly there from birth.

My brother Erin's wife, Nadine, knew a renowned neurosurgeon at Columbia University Medical Center in New York City, Dr. Christopher Winfree, who specialized in surgery for this sort of defect, so I went to see him.

This is the man who's going to be inside my brain, I thought. And here I'd thought I'd already been as intimate with a person as one could be.

"You have a beautiful textbook case," he said. "You're going to need a procedure called posterior fossa decompression. Let's get you in for surgery next week."

So soon? I was terrified.

"What will it entail?" I asked.

"We'll have to shave the back of your head and then make an incision. We'll open the back of the head approximately six inches and permanently remove a little over an inch of your skull. The point is to alleviate the swelling and let the spinal fluid get back to where it needs to be. When the brain has this herniation, the only way to fix it is to get rid of some of the skull to give it room to breathe. Then we'll cauterize the cerebellar tonsils so they'll stop herniating, and we sew on a patch to widen out the dura, which is the protective covering of your brain and spinal column. We leave the patch on there permanently to provide more room for the cerebrospinal fluid to flow."

"Well, that all sounds...horrifying."

"It's not an easy experience, but you should do fine."

"What are the risks involved with a surgery like this?"

"There's surprisingly little risk. With any surgery that involves the brain and spine, there is a risk of nerve damage, but it's a minute risk in this case. There's also a risk that you'll have cerebrospinal fluid leakage, which could require a surgical correction. And, of course, the same risks as you'd have with any surgery with anesthesia: blood clots, stroke..."

I put my head in my hands.

"There are no other options," I said—more of a statement than a question. I knew there was nothing else. This doctor was going to permanently remove a piece of my skull, and I had no real choice but to put my life in his hands and pray that it all would go right.

"You're going to feel a lot better after this surgery is over," he said. "Almost all patients who have this surgery have at least some relief of their symptoms."

"Some?"

"There can be residual symptoms, especially if there's been any spinal cord damage. But let's think positive. Afterward, you'll need to take it easy—you're going to have staples in the back of your head and neck, and it'll be difficult to lift your arms. You'll want to wear very loose clothing until you're healed. Make sure everything buttons in the front and doesn't have to be pulled over your head."

I left there in a haze. It was so much to process. The surgery would be five to six hours long, and then there would be weeks of recovery where I was not allowed to lift anything heavier than five pounds, bend over, do housework, or do anything else that might increase pressure in my head, like straining during a bowel movement or having a prolonged cough (as if I could control that).

Setting the right scene was important to me. I asked a Native American man I knew from Colorado if he would send me a recording of him singing a song I'd heard him perform at a peace conference. He sent me back five minutes of beautiful chanting and singing that I would play through my earbuds in the operating room prior to going under anesthesia.

Before surgery, I drove myself to New York because Paul was working on a big project. The night before I was set to go in, I went to the Palisades Center mall to buy recovery clothing. I started sobbing right there in Neiman Marcus. Sobbing, walking through the pajama racks looking for nightgowns that buttoned in the front. For when I had a *chunk taken out of my skull* and couldn't dress myself. What had I gotten into?

When the time came the following morning, I wanted as much knowledge and control as I could have. I wanted to see the surgical tools and the bed I was going to lie on. I wanted to make eye contact with everyone in that operating room. Instead of being wheeled into the OR, I got permission to walk in and lie down on the table by myself.

"After this is over, you're going to be on a morphine pump," the doctor told me.

"No, I don't want any narcotics."

"Trust me, don't fight this. You're going to want to use it."

They showed me the cage they were going to screw my head into, and the little saws that would cut into my skull. I made a point of talking to everyone. "My name is Colleen," I said to the anesthesiologist, the surgical assistant, the nurses. I wanted them to see me as a person, not just a patient. "Would you please each look me in the eyes and tell me your names, too?"

I'm sure the request surprised them a bit, but they did as I asked.

"I work for AmeriCorps as the director of a teen center. I'm not just a patient. I love to hike and bike."

I hoped that it was enough to make them feel invested in the outcome of this operation, to do their best jobs to ensure I would walk out of that hospital soon to get back to the important work I needed to do.

Then I noticed what was playing on the radio in the OR.

"You're listening to Metallica?" I asked the surgeon.

"Yeah! It's good brain surgery music."

In a way it was reassuring to imagine how confident he had to be to rock out to Metallica while performing major surgery. It was also a funny contrast to my Native American peace song. I put on my earbuds and everything went black.

The next thing I knew, I was waking up in the recovery room with a strange bubbling sensation in the back of my head, like a gurgling stomach—but in my brain. Everything was spinning and I had a hard time focusing or lifting my head. Then came the uncontrollable vomiting. Every time I threw up, the pain in my head was awful. They gave me Zofran for the nausea, and the nurses started pushing the morphine pump for me because I was too out of it to even decide for myself whether or not I needed it.

I stayed in the ICU for two days and then a step-down unit for another two days. Paul came to visit and said, "See? Don't you feel silly that you were so upset?"

Hmm. Not really. I think the occasion of having one's brain cut open is on the list of acceptable things to totally freak out about.

I was allowed to leave after that, but I had to stay at Paul's sister's place near the hospital at least until I got my staples out, two weeks later. Vertigo overtook me in those early days and I had to learn how to balance again. I was on strong steroids to counteract brain swelling, as well as heavy antibiotics, and I began having hallucinations. The bubbling feeling hadn't stopped, and I had visions that spiders were crawling out of the incision in the back of my head. I'd wake up screaming about the bugs—and I could *see* them right there in front of me. It was hard to convince me they weren't real because they were *right there.*

After what felt like eternity but was actually more like a few weeks, everything gradually calmed down, my staples were removed, and I was able to go back home.

Nothing would ever be exactly the same, of course. My surgeon told me that I should never again downhill ski, bungee jump, ride a roller coaster, or do any action sports, because I was always going to be missing part of my skull—which meant I was more prone to serious injury. He had also hollowed out my C1 through C4 vertebrae to make more room for the spinal fluid. If I were to take a significant jolt to the neck, I would have a high risk of spinal injury.

I'd never liked roller coasters anyway, so that one didn't bother me much.

"I can still bike, though, right?" I had asked him. Cycling was so important to me that I couldn't imagine my life without it. In Vermont I had gotten my first mountain bike and road bike, and I loved riding with Paul.

"You can. Just be really careful."

I assured him I would be. I was thrilled that I was starting to get my life back. Being a patient was very difficult for me; I was so used to being active and on the go that it was maddening to have to sit still for weeks. As soon as I was able to, I began waking up with the sun and taking long walks and jogs, thanking God that I was alive and healthy and that the surgeon's promises were coming true. About two months post-surgery, I led a youth hiking trip up to the summit of Camel's Hump, the third-highest mountain in Vermont. For several kids, it was the first time they had ever climbed a mountain. When we got to the summit, we all screamed—and for the first time since my symptoms had started, I didn't get that visceral reaction. No head rush, no feeling like I was going to pass out. It was so freeing and emotional to feel that on top of a mountain surrounded by my kiddos. We looked out over the peak together and I felt such a euphoric joy along with them, just as if it were the first time *I* had summited a mountain, too. I felt such gratitude for something I had taken for granted before. Maybe I would finally be able to put these months of madness behind me.

It meant everything to me to feel almost normal again—not all of my symptoms disappeared, even after months, but probably 90 percent of my migraines were gone, and I didn't have to worry anymore about passing out on the toilet or avoiding sex. Not that I had a whole lot of that going on—my marriage with Paul had been troubled for a while. We had both been working tirelessly for long hours. I now desperately wanted to be a mom, while he still had no desire to be a father. He had stopped saying "I love you" to me, and I could see the look in his eyes change. Our relationship wasn't a romance anymore; it had become something else. We were more like roommates. Friends. The added strain of the surgery and its aftermath was just too much for the tenuous bond between us.

We did go to counseling after the surgery, but when the counselor asked Paul to name what he loved about me, he couldn't think of anything to say. That's when I knew it was time to move on, though we remained friendly.

Maybe I'm just not cut out for relationships, I thought. At thirty-three years old, I was starting to think that the "happy marriage and family" thing was a far-off fantasy that was never going to belong to me. I dove back into my work and tried not to dwell too much. I wanted to be there; the surgeon had predicted my recovery would take six months, but I was at work in three. So, okay, I didn't have my own kids, but I did have "my" kids. A whole slew of them, and they needed me. I bet *they* could have come up with answers to what they loved about me.

Chapter 5

Fate. Destiny. Social Media.

Here was the problem: When my time with AmeriCorps was up, so was my salary with the youth center. The executive director who had hired me said she was just going to close down the center because it was too much work to keep up.

I couldn't let that happen.

Knowing I was going to have to eat and keep a roof over my head, I did the only thing I could possibly do: I kept working there for free. *Just temporarily*, I told myself, until we could find the funding again. I went to a city hall meeting to try to convince the city to take us under their wing and add the center to its budget. We did manage to get St. Albans to bring us into the government's municipality, so that we wouldn't have to pay rent for at least the next year. With the preexisting debt finally paid off, that meant I could start building a sustainable plan that would eventually pay my salary again.

I had always had side jobs anyway, so now those side jobs had to become the "real" jobs. I taught CPR classes with the Red Cross twenty hours a week at places like army bases and corporations, and I received a stipend from a rape crisis center whenever I was called to help on a case. I would have sold fruit on the side of the road just so I could keep working with those kids. They needed me and I needed them. We kept each other moving. If that meant I had to live in a minimalistic fashion, I was okay with that.

Fighting for our center's survival was an opportunity to teach the kids about advocacy as well. If we wanted public funding, one way to handle it was to get onto town ballots so that a percentage of funding meant for youth services could go toward our youth center. The kids would come with me to town hall meetings and we'd give presentations about what kind of difference we were making, with numbers to back it up. We learned about crime rates in all the area towns and how the center was making a long-term viable impact on crime reduction and improving educational outcomes. It was empowering for the kids to speak up for themselves and the center they loved. They helped to keep it running as much as I did.

I loved our trips together, and I loved staying active with them. Health problems still plagued me, though, long after the brain surgery had passed. I kept getting fevers and having digestive problems, along with extreme joint pain and fatigue. I couldn't seem to regulate my temperature—my body wouldn't shiver in the cold to warm me back up, and in the summer my hands would turn purple and swollen. Once again it was back to doctors for a battery of tests, none of which came back conclusive for anything.

On and off, I battled depression because of the health issues, my loneliness after the end of a marriage, and some days for no solid reason at all. Sometimes depression is just like that. You're in a funk and you don't really know why. It's just this cloud that grays out everything in your view.

I had good days and bad, good months and bad. Getting on my bike helped on the days I could do that, and being with the kids helped. Going to peace conferences and being inspired by the PeaceJam Nobel laureates helped. Ruminating about how I was probably going to be alone forever and marriage was a sham and maybe I was fundamentally unlovable did *not* help.

Then along came a reminder that was both sweet and wistful.

I had just signed on to my computer when I saw the notification in July 2008:

Sean Alexander wants to be friends on Facebook.

How many times had I thought about contacting him? In fact, I had tried looking him up in the phone book a few times over the years, but he had moved and Sean Alexander is a common name. Now here he was in my inbox, and my heart skipped a beat before I even checked out his profile.

Then there he was. And he was still hot.

What stunned me was that I was his only friend...the very first person he'd friend-requested when he signed up. That felt so good. After all these years, he hadn't forgotten about me, either.

How many years had it been, anyway? I did some quick math and came up with seventeen. Nearly two decades. So much had gone on since then that I had no idea whether either of us was even the same person anymore. According to his profile, he lived in Colorado. I stared and stared, trying to figure out whether he was married (it didn't say in his sparse profile), and spotted a ring in one of his pictures.

That was probably for the best—I wasn't looking for a relationship, and this basically took that off the table. Still, I had long felt like he was "the one who got away." It would be so nice to reconnect and just hear his voice again, maybe get the chance to apologize for breaking up with him with no explanation all those years earlier.

"Blast from the past!" he wrote. "What are you doing in Vermont?"

I took a deep breath and sent him a message:

I have always wanted to apologize to you. As a teen, I was heavily brainwashed by religion. I was fearful of being in any relationship with anyone who did not share my same values with salvation. Thank you for being a respectful friend/boyfriend. I appreciated it. Now as an adult, I work with many youths with paths heavily saturated by drug use, sexual abuse, domestic violence, and even a brainwashed-by-religion teen who are transitioning into adolescence and trying to understand their boundaries and the world around them under such a small microscope. I love people and advocating for people.

I have been working for a youth center and running a program called PeaceJam based out of Denver here in Vermont. This

September I'll be heading to LA to an international peace conference with the kids. I have no children but instead work with them. I have become an independent female.

Basically, I wanted to say thank you, as you were a pivotal part in the development of my psyche as an adolescent and many of our conversations pertaining to your love of the ocean and the outdoors and how that brought you closer to God more so than attending church stuck with me and percolated into my early adulthood.

I'm so happy to see you online and to see your big smile, and to know you are well and enjoying life.

We wrote back and forth a couple of times, enough for me to find out that he wasn't married after all. The ring was just for fun. (It was on his right hand in the photo, which I probably should have noticed.) He was working at a restaurant now, and had traded in his surfboard for a snowboard.

Even knowing he was single, though, I didn't want to connect too heavily with him right away. My marriage was just ending and the last thing I needed was to get into another relationship.

I messaged him with my phone number so we could catch up, but he didn't call for a few weeks. One day, he was mountain biking and when he hit the summit at 11,000 feet, he decided he was going to call me. I saw the Colorado area code and took a breath before picking up the phone, hoping it was him.

"Hey, Colleen," he said with a smile in his voice.

"Hey, you!"

"What are you doing?"

"Just got home from work. What about you?"

"I'm on top of a mountain. I was cycling up here and thinking about you and I thought... 'You know, I'm just gonna call her.'"

He sounded just the same, only manlier. We spoke for about twenty-five minutes, both keeping our cool about how excited we were to talk to each other. It was just a nice, warm conversation. Just like that first date, he felt so familiar, so much like home.

I learned more about the years since I'd last seen him. After he graduated from college, he did a short stint as a model for big companies like Calvin Klein and Hugo Boss, so I guess he had finally realized how good-looking he was. He was also dating a model then, but they broke up when he realized she was cheating on him with someone in the business. Pretty quickly, he realized the modeling world really wasn't his style, and he had hightailed it out of there to become the bachelor of Vail.

Within weeks, we were talking on the phone all the time, sometimes until the sun came up. I began dreaming about him, but not sexual dreams... which was interesting, because I was very much a sexual creature by then. I fantasized instead about snuggling into his chest and falling asleep. It was as PG-rated as our high school relationship had been. After about the third time, I thought, *Something is seriously wrong with me*. This beautiful man, and my biggest fantasy involved us being fully clothed?

It is just a fantasy, though, I reminded myself. He was in Colorado. I was done with relationships. It was nothing more than a fun imagination about what might have been.

Real life kept intruding on my imaginary one; in real life, I was still going back and forth to doctors and still getting no answers.

It wasn't celiac disease. Not Crohn's. It wasn't related to the Chiari malformation.

"Maybe I'm just burned out," I sighed to one of my girlfriends on the phone.

"You need to get away. When was the last time you took a vacation?"

Hmm. In the nineties?

Maybe she was right.

Chapter 6

Costa Rica

On the recommendation of a couple of girlfriends, I decided to book a trip to a yoga retreat in Guanacaste, Costa Rica. Friends of mine who were yoga enthusiasts had recommended the instructor, and I looked forward to getting away and clearing my mind. I liked the idea of taking my first real solo trip. I called the number listed on her website and asked to come in November.

"I'm familiar with your work and I'm glad to have you here," she told me. "But we're normally not open in November—it's the rainy season."

"Oh," I said. I told her about what was going on in my life—about the brain surgery and the end of my long relationship and how unsettled I felt.

"If you just want to do a personal retreat, you're welcome to come," she said. "You'd basically be alone, except for my son and the gardener and the man who takes care of the horses. And the person who makes the cheese!"

"That sounds great. I would love to be alone for a while. I just need a place to relax, do lots of yoga, and have some good organic food."

"We can certainly provide that. You'll have a queen-sized bed and an open-air kitchen."

She offered me a room for forty-nine dollars a night, which—I mean, honestly, how could I resist? I booked it for seven nights.

When I told Sean about my trip, he threw me a curveball.

"I might be in Costa Rica then, too," he said.

"Really?"

"I always go to either Costa Rica or Nicaragua in November to surf during the slow season at the resorts."

I knew what he was not-so-subtly hinting, and it was exciting and terrifying. He wanted to meet me in Costa Rica.

I can't let him be my Eat, Pray, Love. *He can't be my pool boy*, I thought. It was too soon. If we met, I wouldn't be able to resist him, and it would be a rebound thing. He deserved better than that.

Then I thought about it again and decided that I was a strong woman who could handle keeping her desires in check. The opportunity to see him again was so unexpected and exciting, even if it was tempered by a lot of anxious overthinking.

Sean arrived in Costa Rica first. He came to pick me up at the airport, and as soon as he spotted me, he came running over for a hug. I was wearing a big backpack. He must have bear-hugged my backpack for ten minutes before I finally broke free and put it down so we could hug unencumbered.

It was pretty late when Sean picked me up, and it seemed like too much to make the two- to three-hour drive through the rain forest to get to where I was staying, so we made the decision to stay locally and put off the drive until the morning. We arrived at a nearby hotel and I asked for two rooms.

"Why do you want two rooms?" the receptionist asked.

"Yeah!" Sean said with a big smile. "Why do you want two rooms?"

"No, we definitely need two rooms," I told her.

I turned to Sean and quietly said, "That's not what this trip is about. The purpose of this trip is for me to just be. I can't jump into something. And plus, you live in Colorado..."

"Well, I have three rooms left. Two in smoking, one in nonsmoking," the woman told us.

You have to be kidding me, I thought. It was like a movie scene with an all-too-convenient obstacle to advance the plot. Neither of us wanted to be in the smoking wing.

Sean looked at me with that big, silly grin again.

I threw my hands in the air. One room. Fine.

It was about the Costa Rican equivalent of a Super 8. After settling into our perfectly adequate room, we went out for food and stared at each other. The last version of Sean I'd seen was eighteen. Pieces of him were the same—his shiny hair, his freckles, his eyes—but there were wonderful new lines around his eyes, and a new brow line.

He's an adult, I thought. *A full-grown man.* And that made me take a moment to assess myself and realize...*I, too, am an adult now.*

We went for a night swim afterward, and Sean reminded me that we used to sneak into hotel pools back in high school. My eyes drifted to a scar on his abdomen. He looked down as he started to explain.

"I got into an accident on my snowboard three years ago. I was by myself on a new board in the back country and the front of my board hit a tree branch covered in deep snow. I went end over end and got impaled by another tree branch."

"Holy crap."

"Yeah, it was pretty bad. I had to pull the branch out of my body and crawl back to the path to find help. I was bleeding all over the place."

"You could have died!"

"I could have. I needed a lot of blood transfusions—and a colostomy. That was no fun."

I didn't know what to say. The thought that he could have been gone before we ever got the chance to reconnect hit me so hard. I didn't want to let him go. We stood there hugging in the shallow end until a worker came and told us in Spanish that it was after hours and time for us to get out. Then we stayed up in our room and talked all night long.

The following morning he drove me to the yoga retreat center, where I spent a couple of days before we were to meet up again in the village where Sean was surfing. On my retreat, I went horseback riding and spent many, many hours reading and lying in a hammock in addition to doing yoga.

The retreat owner's son drove me in his old Toyota 4Runner to meet Sean. We arrived first, and I got out of the passenger side. The driver thought I had cleared the car—but I hadn't. My foot was still in the truck's path when he began driving, music blasting through the speakers.

CRUNCH!

He ran over my foot, and I let out a howl—which caused him to panic and throw the truck into reverse and run over it a second time. Everyone around us began screaming.

"Grab my back!" I yelled to a bystander in the limited Spanish I knew, because I was afraid I was about to pass out. Lots of people crowded around, wanting to help, but no one knew what to do. Luckily, I'd been an EMT. I barked out orders, roughly translated. "Lower me down to the ground. Elevate my foot."

Just as this commotion was happening, Sean rounded the corner. He got out of the car and said, "What the hell happened?"

The pain was ridiculous. I was sure my foot was broken. Sean rushed me to the nearest hospital—two hours away—and it wasn't exactly like hospitals back home. Here, the hallways were all open-air, and the X-ray room was across from the morgue. The X-ray technician gabbed on her cell phone in Spanish and finished smoking her cigarette before putting me through.

We were supposed to be at the beach, I thought.

We had to tell them that Sean was my brother (*"¡Mi hermano!"*) so they'd let him stay with me. The doctor looked at my X-rays and said that no bones were broken; I should just stay off the foot and take antibiotics. That was it; no one cleaned my foot or even picked the gravel out of it.

I was lucky that we hadn't been on a paved road and that it had been rainy season, because while the tire had pretty well mangled the top of my foot, my foot had sunk into the sand gravel, which protected it from being a lot worse. Later, when I got back home to my own doctors, I would find out that I did have a hairline fracture—but I didn't know that yet, and so I just figured I'd do the best I could to get through the pain.

But how on Earth was I supposed to do a yoga retreat? Forget it—there was no point in my going back. Sean suggested taking me out for margaritas to dull the pain, and luckily the retreat owner was understanding of my plight…particularly because it was her son who ran over my foot.

The closest lodging was a four-leaf eco-rated luxury hotel in the thick of the rain forest in Arenal for $400 a night, which neither of us had—but we did have credit cards. We stayed there for three lovely nights, and during the day, I mostly lay down with my foot elevated or we did whatever limited activities we could that didn't involve much walking. We visited geothermal hot springs from the runoff water of a volcano, which felt so healing. When the clouds cleared, you could see steam from the still-active Arenal volcano. Then there were the toucans and howler monkeys. It was a magical atmosphere.

Throughout it all I tried to understand what was happening with Sean and me. I had such strong feelings for him, but I had already decided that it wasn't a healthy choice to be in a relationship at that time—and neither did I want it to be a random, hot "hookup" with a blast from the past. Yet being with him was so genuine and loving, effortlessly fun and free. I had to keep telling myself to stop getting caught up in the moment, though, because it was all going to go away soon.

Come on. He lives in Colorado, and you have way too much going on in your life.

But a second thought would compete with that one, and before long I was having inner conversations with God about what I was supposed to do.

You must have put me here for a reason, and if you meant for me to be here reconnecting with Sean, then I don't want to screw it up.

Finally we were back at the airport; I was flying home to Vermont and he to Colorado. It was an emotionally devastating moment for both of us, dealing with the sudden reality that we were going to be two thousand miles apart tomorrow and that even though we just wanted to skip out on our lives and get on a plane together, that wasn't a rational choice.

The whole ride home, though, all I could think was *How long do I have to wait?*

When would I feel right about being in a new relationship? This wasn't a rebound. He was like the other part of me, and not the annoying part. How often does that come around? Never, that's when.

About seventy-two hours after I got home, I booked a flight on Priceline to visit him for New Year's Eve. Then I called him.

"Hey, what are you doing for New Year's Eve?"

"I think I'm working. Why?"

"Is it all right if I come out?"

"Uh...yeah, that would be great."

"Good, because I already bought a ticket."

That Christmas I spent time with old friends from high school who asked what I was so smiley about. I told them I had seen Sean again.

"That's so cool! You two were always meant to be together!" one of my friends said—which just fueled the fire. *She is wise. She must be right.*

I flew into Denver a week later. I had never been to Colorado before, and it had the same fairy-tale effect on me that Costa Rica did. On our drive to Sean's house in Vail, the high peaks across the skyline were so beautiful that I felt like I was in a storybook. He held my hand from the driver's seat and I nearly had to pinch myself.

I'm in Sean Alexander's car, and this time, there aren't even holes in the floorboard.

There was one hitch, though.

It's not a very environmentally friendly car.

Well, you can't win 'em all.

The powder snow glistened in the sun, and I soaked in everything about both the atmosphere and my companion. We went to his company party, where his coworkers asked what kind of magic I had worked on this perpetual bachelor.

It was only a three-day trip, but we packed in a lot of quality time hiking and going out to eat and playing in the snow. This time I didn't hesitate to share his room. Soon after my trip ended, Sean called me to tell me that he had booked a flight to come visit me in March. It went on like that for about ten months, with our back-and-forth visits. By then there was a staff at the youth center and most of my work was writing grants, which I could do remotely as long as I had someone to manage the place.

We were walking through the woods near his house once when he said, "Did you know that the aspen tree roots are one of the oldest living root systems in the world? They sprawl miles and miles and they're all interconnected. It's like the way we're so deeply connected all the way across the miles, too."

All of the *shouldn't*s in my mind melted off. This was real. It wasn't going away. I was supposed to be with Sean.

At dinner we held hands and thanked God for our unity. "We ask for your guidance in this process. Help us be mindful of our lives on this Earth and our lives with each other."

Not long after that, he called me up on the phone and said, "I'm done. I want to move to Vermont."

"You're going to hate it here. It rains all the time, the snow is not fluffy, and the mountains are not high peaks," I said.

"I don't care. I love you, and that is where I need to be."

I was so terrified of ruining everything. Until this point, our relationship had been in short spurts. I knew full well that living together was very different from spending weekends together every month or two. My tiny cabin was already overcrowded—there wasn't a lot of room for a six-foot-four guy in there with me and a dog and cat. Yet we drove across the country together in his Isuzu Rodeo packed with all his belongings like a 3-D version of Tetris. He is stunningly adept at organization.

We traveled well together for those four or five days, which I thought was a good sign—because being stuck in an SUV for days on end where there isn't any room to blink in the midst of summer heat can really teach you what you're made of. Sure enough, the move worked very organically; only the cat was suspicious of this intruder. We fell into our new lives together with amazing ease.

And then he proposed.

Chapter 7

The Big Move

W E WERE IN DAYTONA visiting family when he got down on one knee in the same garden where we took our prom pictures, and I felt so giddy.

As we made our plans to get married in Florida near where we grew up, we wanted to do something fun to mark our new life together. We were both athletic and loved to ride bikes and run as a pair, but neither of us had done a triathlon before. We were thinking it over and surfing the internet for honeymoon ideas when we found that there was going to be a triathlon in a place called Honeymoon Island in Florida in June 2010.

"We should do that. We should train ourselves and do that and get married. It'll be super fun."

I was kidding—at least mostly. We were newly engaged, back in wintertime Vermont, and the triathlon was only six months away. Sean lightheartedly agreed with me, and I'm not sure if either one of us was actually serious about the idea...yet for some crazy reason, a couple of weeks later, we went ahead and signed up. Which meant that we were going to have to train for the triathlon and plan our wedding quickly.

Then a bit of reality set in when we tried to swim together for the first time at the gym. We both barely made it one lap. Neither of us had any technique. We hired a coach who trained us a few times a week, and after the first couple of sessions, we both agreed: *This was a bad idea.* We were not swimmers, and there wasn't much time to *become* swimmers.

Still, slowly but surely, we were able to do more and more laps. The goal was to make it eighteen lengths of the pool without stopping. We'd have to replicate that in the ocean, then bike fifteen miles and run a 5K. We practiced at and around the gym until we finally gained confidence.

"We can so do this," I announced.

"We're going to nail this," Sean agreed.

And then we got there, and we were wrong. That triathlon kicked our butts.

We had heat exhaustion and sunburns and we thought we would collapse, but we finished. It was humbling, but we got it done. Then we headed to Daytona to prepare for our wedding before friends and family showed up.

My parents really liked Sean, and my father smiled and said, "The first two were just practice for the perfect one," as he walked me down the aisle. He knew, at last, that I had gotten it right this time.

This meant so much to me, and the tears rolled down my face before I even saw my husband-to-be standing on the beach. Making my father proud was always of utmost importance to me.

It was not the ornate spectacle that my first wedding had been, for sure. We stood barefoot on a quiet stretch of beach with two bagpipers leading us in and a friend serving as our minister; my bridesmaids wore navy-blue sundresses and the guys wore tropical shirts and linen pants and it was just perfect.

About fifty close friends and family members stood in a circle around us. Our vows were written on pieces of birch bark that we had collected while hiking in Vermont, and our song was "In My Arms" by Jon Foreman—a song that encapsulated what it was like to live apart for the early part of our relationship and wait for the day we could finally be together.

At the reception, an entire pipe-and-drum corps played for us in return for $300 and half a keg of Guinness. They were more than an amazing gift to our day. After going over our wedding a hundred times in my head, there is nothing I would do any differently.

Later that night, I put out my arm, touched my wedding ring to Sean's, and said, "Wonder Twin powers, activate!"

He cracked up. It became our *thing*.

Soon after our wedding, I got a terrific new job offer. The northeast regional director of PeaceJam wanted to hire me to work directly for the organization as a program manager because they'd seen how well I'd grown the division in Vermont. I loved the program so much and was honored to hear how impressed they were with me. I was making a salary again, but this would be a financial step forward and a continuation of the type of work I was already doing and enjoying: helping to lead programs and conferences, raising money for scholarships, giving talks, writing press releases... stuff that was right in my wheelhouse.

It would mean moving to their headquarters in Connecticut, though. I didn't know a whole lot about Connecticut, but it was still the northeast—how different could it be? And it appealed to me that Sean and I could get a start in a new place together. Colorado had been Sean's and Vermont had been mine; instead of always feeling like Sean had moved to unfamiliar ground for me, maybe Connecticut would feel like *ours*. It could be a place where we could have some firsts together. I checked in with him.

"I think it's a great opportunity. Let's do this," he said.

"What will you do there?"

"Maybe substitute teach. Anything but the restaurant industry. I think I can dust off my résumé and figure it out."

The only thing left to consider was that I was leaving the teen center behind. I'd been there for eight years, and that was a hard thing to think about. The kids there felt like *my* kids or nieces and nephews. It was a time when social media was in full swing, though, and I reasoned that I could still stay in touch with them—many of whom weren't even kids anymore. In the years since I'd started, some of "my kids" had already graduated from college and started careers of their own, gotten married, had children...it was amazing to watch them bloom.

Things were so much more organized, too. We had a staff and a team of volunteers who were capable of carrying on the good work we'd done, I knew. So I tearfully wrote up a letter to give notice of my resignation almost ten weeks in advance because I wanted them to have plenty of time to hire someone good to take over as executive director, and so I could have a hand in training my replacement. I was assured that this would happen, and then I got called into the city manager's office.

"Since you're leaving," he explained matter-of-factly, "it seems like a feasible time for us to phase out the center because it's not a good financial asset for the city budget."

I burst into tears. "It's not *meant* to be a source of financial income. It's meant to help the city's youth."

"We still have to be responsible to our taxpayers..."

"This *is* responsible. It's as responsible as you can get! It provides a place for kids to be during non-school hours. We have proof that the youth participating at the center are having less truancy at school, teenage pregnancy has declined, teen arrests and violations around the city have declined, and I can show you teachers' comments that our students are more positively involved in learning and social interaction. We're making a difference!"

"I understand this is hard. Sometimes hard decisions have to be made."

I sat there in stunned silence, choking on my tears. I had no power here, no standing.

"What's going to happen to the center?" I managed when I found my voice again.

"The school is going to rent the space that the city owns and use it for varsity basketball. They're *paying* to rent it."

"When?"

"Next week."

"*Next week?*"

We had done so much good in that place. What we had not done, however, was present a pretty, privileged place for the upper-echelon youth of Franklin County to attend. We hadn't been working with the old-money parents of the community; we were working with a lot of families on welfare, broken families, and students who were not all varsity athletes. As the city manager beamed about the athletic community, it occurred to me that our population wasn't the city government's priority.

Soon, they would professionally paint over every wall that the kids had spent months painting from ceiling to floor one summer. They would strip the entire space that had been built with love, sweat, and tears, and sterilize it for a profitable income revenue.

"You cannot leave these kids with nothing," I said.

"We won't. We're in talks with the Supervisory Union to establish a new program. We just need to figure out how to make it profitable, but we'll work with the kids and find a way to reopen in a new place in a few months."

A couple of days later, I was sitting there in the center, trying to figure out how I was supposed to tell the kids, when a former student walked in for a visit from college. She was all smiles, ready to tell me about her classes and her roommate, but when she asked how I was doing, I couldn't fake it.

"They're closing us down in a few days," I said.

"For real?"

I nodded and burst into tears all over again. I felt like such a traitor.

We planned a goodbye party for the center, and a city representative came in to tell the kids the same thing he'd told me: that this wasn't the end. That they would return stronger, bigger than ever. I wanted so much to believe that.

A week after my last day, I came back to an empty center. Blank walls, no furniture, no files, no music equipment...it was all just gone. Paul showed up, too, and burst into tears. It was the end of an era for each of us, and the pain I felt seeing it stripped bare was awful. Would they have closed that center if I hadn't resigned? I'll never know. Maybe it would have happened just the same; maybe it would have taken a little longer. Maybe I could have saved it. It still haunts me.

I started work for PeaceJam Northeast on October 1, 2010, while still going through terrible anxiety over the closing of the youth center, and the stress of putting together our lives in a new state. I often felt like I was hovering over my body, watching myself as if life were a movie instead of reality. I kept having a recurring dream of my dry, older hands on my bike handlebars, and then a heavy force would come over me and I would die.

"I think I'm going to die on a bike," I told Sean, who tried to reassure me. It was just another in a series of empathic visions and dreams that felt very real, which sure didn't help my anxiety.

One of my first priorities after moving was to find a good therapist, which I did. I went every week.

My office in Hartford was an hour from where we lived on the beautiful Connecticut shoreline. I was now working with gang members and hearing on a daily basis about people getting knifed and shot. Despite my background working with troubled youth, the bar was completely different here. It was relatively easy doing social work in Vermont; here there was much more of everything—teen pregnancy, depression, suicide, hard drugs, violence. I dealt with a lot more mental illness and drug addiction than I ever had before.

The other thing that made it so difficult for me was the great chasm here between the haves and the have-nots. I grew up in a middle-class area where people were friendly to one another. You just waved at everyone you passed—that was normal. Here, if you waved and smiled at people, they'd stare at you like, *What the hell do you want? Why are you smiling at me?*

People drove too fast and rushed through life, and I didn't understand why even the wealthy people seemed so stressed out all the time. Driving through the crazy interstate corridor to Hartford, I would question myself, *What gives me the right to do this work? I've never been in a gang. I don't know anything about the Latin Kings. I don't know how to connect with this at all.*

I worried that I had made a huge mistake in moving here.

In order to make a difference, I had to shed my own insecurities about being privileged and inadequate, and that was a process. It took a long time to feel that when I went to lead these teachings from our curriculum to audiences that ran the gamut from community centers that welcomed youth from all backgrounds to upscale private boarding schools, I was capable of bringing something relevant and meaningful to their lives.

I'd take the kids to these peace conferences in different states to discuss what they learned and how they could connect it to their lives and the issues in their communities. One of the cool parts was that I roped in a few of my Vermont kids who were now college students to come as mentors.

Within the conferences, students are broken into "family groups" of about twenty-five, and often there are kids grouped together from very different backgrounds. I watched some of them go through transformations more extreme than mine in just the course of a weekend. Some would meet each other and think, *I have no idea how to talk to you. We're totally different,* and by the end of the conference, they'd be hugging it out and saying, "I love you and I can't wait to stay in touch with you."

We even had students from a school for the deaf attend some of the conferences with translators, and their reactions were always wonderful.

"This is one of the coolest things we do all year," one of the kids told a program assistant. "Usually we're just around deaf kids all the time and we feel ostracized, but then we come to a conference like this and we're not singled out as different. We're treated like everyone else."

I stressed out about how to incorporate the conference environment into these kids' daily lives, which were nowhere near as sheltered and safe. I wanted them to have the same kinds of outcomes as my Vermont kids, who overwhelmingly were going to college and doing well.

My stomach was in knots about it, which only exacerbated my ongoing health problems. After all the testing, I'd finally gotten a diagnosis: lupus.

Lupus isn't easy to diagnose, and usually gets named only by process of eliminating all the other likely options.

It's a chronic inflammatory disease that causes the body's immune system to lose the ability to differentiate between good and bad. Your immune system attacks your own tissues and organs, and it can cause a whole range of symptoms like the ones I'd been experiencing—serious fatigue, joint pain, digestive problems, headaches, fever, light sensitivity, anemia, swelling...it's a disease that flares up at times and goes into remission at others, which explained why I was often perfectly fine and able to be active, then flattened on the couch other days. Some people have fairly mild cases, while others have it much worse than I did.

On top of that, I was also diagnosed with cryoglobulinemia, a rare condition where abnormal proteins clump together in my blood vessels in cold weather and cause the plasma to thicken like syrup. That can block off blood vessels and cause gangrene in fingers and toes. Awesome.

All I can tell you is that with all these things combined, this was a dark period in my life. I now knew I had multiple serious and incurable health conditions, including an autoimmune disease, and that any of them could actually kill me.

It was *work* to get myself out of bed and moving each day, to remind myself that it would do no good to stay stuck in despair. I had to find something positive to motivate me. Often, that involved the kids, both from the youth center and from the new program.

Gail, my "little sister" from St. Albans, had finished her associate's degree in fire science and had gone on to a two-year paramedic program, and Sean and I drove to Maine that May to be at her graduation.

When she walked into the party after the ceremony, she didn't even know that we had driven up to be there. She saw us and everything brightened. Later, she told us that it was a defining moment for her—*These are the people who believe in me. Family is what you make it.*

That month, we also organized a special event to celebrate Green Up Day and get to know our neighbors. Green Up Day, specific to Vermont, is similar to Earth Day and focuses on cleaning up and improving the environment. I had participated every year in Vermont, gathering up crews to clean garbage out of walking trails or kayak out into the Lake Champlain basin and bag up the trash we found. In our Connecticut town, we found people to be pretty hermit-like, not socializing with one another around the neighborhood beyond simple hellos. It's hard to get into drawn-out conversations in the winter, but now that spring had come, it felt like the time to change that.

Ospreys had returned to the salt marsh that ran through our backyard to nest and canvass for prey, swooping down over the shallow water and coming up with fish in their beaks. It was fascinating to watch—but whenever low tide came, a much sadder sight arose: lots and lots of human-made garbage in this natural habitat.

Sometimes things like that feel like *other* people's things—let someone else take care of it. But I had learned that you can always feel better by taking charge of your own surroundings to whatever extent you can. Regardless of who was responsible or who made the mess, if you have the power to make it better, do it. I reached out to the town and asked if they could drop off a Dumpster at the end of our street so I could organize a cleanup event. The person who answered the phone thought I was nuts, but sure enough, a Dumpster arrived.

Sean and I typed up a letter to distribute to our neighbors:

Hello! We are your new neighbors, Sean and Colleen, and we moved here recently from Vermont. We are writing with an invitation.

Did you know May 7 is Green Up Day? We want to help clean up our watershed and our sound, and we're asking you to join us. Afterwards, we'll have a clambake and beer at our house.

We printed about thirty invitations and put them in our neighbors' mailboxes. On that day, about twelve neighbors showed up. We'd never met any of them before and most of them hadn't met one another. We shook hands with everyone, handed out contractor bags and gloves, and headed out together to start picking up trash. It went so well that we basically had to tell everyone to go home at the end of the night because they were all still gabbing and drinking on the porch and we had to go to bed.

My biggest focus at that time was preparing for the bike tour Cycling for Peace, which was my harebrained fundraising idea. It was a huge ride through our northeast territory: starting in Connecticut, going up through Providence, Rhode Island; zigzagging through Massachusetts to Saratoga, New York; Brattleboro, Vermont; Merrimack, New Hampshire; Portsmouth, New Hampshire; and finalizing the trip in Portland, Maine. Sean would join me for the first leg, but then he would have to go back to work. My sister-in-law Kaori would make the whole trip with me, though.

Months of planning went into it. The purpose of the ride was to promote awareness about PeaceJam by doing public talks and community events and sending out press releases in the areas we cycled through. Along the way I would also give talks and interact with the PeaceJam youth in those areas, exploring what inspired them and how they were creating change within their communities. There seemed no better way to promote PeaceJam than by doing this endeavor on a bicycle, fueled only by my legs, lungs, and heart.

But I hadn't counted on quite so much . . . *weather*.

We began at seven a.m. on September 19, 2011, riding for eight hours against strong headwinds. I struggled with the cold, buying warmer arm sleeves on our arrival at our first destination. Then there was lots of rain and fog, and steep climbs up mountain ranges. Every time we arrived at our next stop, we were wet, cold, muddy, and exhausted, yet every nightly event recharged us. It was inspiring to meet so many other adults and kids who were working toward the same goals, and to find out what they were doing to make an impact in their areas, like bringing Special Olympics to their county or helping a school reduce the amount of waste it generates. We drove back to Connecticut feeling totally spent and excited about what we had accomplished, in terms of raising both awareness and money. At the end of the ride, Kaori and I had biked close to six hundred miles in six days through six states. Not a single issue. It was such a blessing to visit all of these PeaceJam sites and speak across the region where I worked.

Little by little, I found my groove and my passion at PeaceJam Northeast, and I started organizing workshops and roundtable discussions on the issues that we needed to talk about—things like teen pregnancy and suicide. Eventually I realized that the issues may have been on different scales, but there was still so much that connects all of us.

Six months into my new life in Connecticut, I finally felt like I was getting my act together. Sean, who had struggled to find work, picked up a temporary job as a mail carrier, too. We got hooked on triathlons and trained together during our free time, planning for the next race and the next. I started feeling more like myself again. *Maybe it wasn't a bad decision to move here after all,* I thought.

Chapter 8

Flatlining

Nᴇᴀʀʟʏ ᴏɴᴇ ʏᴇᴀʀ ᴛᴏ the day after starting my new job, I left a package of turkey to defrost on the counter, gave Sean a kiss, and headed out for a work meeting. It was Saturday morning, and though my hours were normally Monday to Friday, this kind of job required flexibility—what we were doing with PeaceJam was important, and I didn't mind putting in weekend and evening hours when we were preparing for conferences or planning special projects. I felt very lucky to do the kind of work I did.

There had been another good change, too—a few months back they'd moved my office out of Hartford and to the shoreline. In Hartford, there had been no way I could ride a bike to work, but now riding was possible, though not ideal. I'd hemmed and hawed about the idea.

"I don't know," I had said to Sean. "It's still a pretty busy road."

"Well, let's scope it out and see."

So we took the ride together probably twenty times, noting where there were possible hazards. The trip there and back was a straight shot on Boston Post Road—no turns or stop signs, just a few traffic lights. Even so, you don't get to mentally check out when you're a road cyclist. You have to be constantly vigilant, watching for the various things that could hurt you or your bike. Potholes, gravel, roadwork, traffic...I took bike safety seriously and stayed on guard.

By the day of this meeting, I'd been biking in most days for about two months. It was a twelve-mile commute to and from work, and I did it on my favorite bike—my Jamis Coda. We had been together for almost ten years. She was all steel with a carbon fiber fork. I had her converted to a touring bike with dropped handlebars, and she rode like warm butter on a skillet.

Planet Fitness was right next to my office, and I kept a membership there so I could take showers after my rides in to work. While I was there, I stopped to make a quick Facebook post:

Just finished biking to work, light jacket and leg warmers, sunny skies...I wonder how much longer I can get away with biking? Hoping for at least another month of this!

After a shower, I was refreshed and ready to meet with my supervisor. We were there to talk about my recent Cycling for Peace tour.

"Looks like you raised about three thousand dollars toward scholarships," he said.

"And spoke to about a thousand people. Yes, it was a very successful ride."

"I want you to know that I've gotten very positive feedback from both students and teachers about your talks, and it's led to great press in several papers. Have you seen the articles yet?"

"Just one or two."

"Well, there's a lot more than that. Our division is doing well with your work and you're due a raise soon…"

My ears perked up. I knew they did cost-of-living increases.

"Thank you. I still don't have a new contract, though. Is that coming soon?"

My contract was for one year, and I'd been asking for weeks about when a new contract would be forthcoming.

"Yes, sorry for the delay. I'll have the new contract for you within the week. Your job is secure here for the next three to four years."

What a relief! I'd figured my job was safe, but it was nice to hear it said out loud.

Sean and I had just decided to start trying to have a baby, so it was even better to hear that I wasn't going to have to figure out how to afford diapers when the time came. It was such an exciting time; I felt like I was finally where I wanted to be in life. In fact, I was hoping I was already pregnant and carrying our first baby! We had been trying that entire month and it felt like the time was right.

Two hours after the meeting started, I was back outside on my bike again, in my fluorescent gear: cycling shorts, a bright yellow Pearl Izumi top, and a highlighter-yellow cycling jacket. Even my bike panniers were bright yellow. I pulled on my Giro Livestrong helmet with its fluorescent streaks, clicked my cycling shoes into the pedals, pulled on my bike gloves, and headed off. I always made a point to dress as brightly and safely colored as possible.

October 8, 2011, could not have been a more perfect fall day in Connecticut. When I rode toward home at eleven a.m., the sun was brilliant in the blue sky, and a light breeze tickled my arms. The leaves were just starting to change colors and fall gracefully to the ground, peppering my view with gorgeous oranges, reds, and yellows. I pitied the car commuters a bit; they were completely missing out on the sea air, the chirping birds, the meditative feeling of pedaling on such a clear day. Fall has always been my favorite season. Pumpkins, pumpkin lattes, pumpkin cookies, pumpkin ale...what could be better?

I even liked the way fall was a harbinger of winter. The changing of the literal seasons made me think about the changing of the seasons in my own life. Riding past a stretch of beautiful historic homes and buildings and an old-timey general store, I had a sense of peace.

I settled into the side lane and imagined how excited my dog would be to see me when I got home. Sedona was already an old girl by then, but ever enthusiastic. She'd bark and wag her tail when I came through the door, then we'd hug and wrestle before I'd take her out for a walk. Sean was at work doing postal deliveries, so I'd made plans with a good friend for a nice, long ride later that afternoon.

But I would never make it there.

As I continued on my straight path, I saw a freight truck turning in my direction from a side street. He was just feet away from the stop sign, coming fast, and I briefly made eye contact with the driver. There wasn't even time in my brain for me to put through the complete thought: *Oh, God. He's coming right at me. Stop!*

He briefly slowed at the corner, but then the engine revved up again and he accelerated right through, right toward me.

It's too fast. There is nothing I can do but scream as the giant truck knocks me down onto my left side, my legs momentarily tangled up with my bike. I hear snapping and grinding.

Why?

He runs over me with his front tires, rolling my body over and flipping me to the other side. I feel my insides cracking. Then he runs over me with his back tires. I'm rolled into the middle of the street and I'm pretty sure this could be my last moment on Earth. The shadow of the truck disappears.

Why did he kill me? He looked right at me.

My abdomen, my legs, the whole left side of my body... everything is on fire, everything is in desperate pain and so heavy. Blood gushes out from multiple wounds, and all I can do is scream and scream.

HELP!

I'm able to raise my head enough to see something bright white and yellow protruding from my leg. It's bone, tendons, and fatty cells.

I hear the truck accelerate, like I'd been nothing more than a speed bump. The driver attempts to flee the scene, but someone stops him. It felt like just me and the leaves only a few moments earlier, but people come rushing from all directions now. I hear, "Oh my God, she's alive."

Am I? Alive, I realize, but barely. The skin has peeled right off most of the lower half of my body, along with my clothing—my shorts are shredded off and my shirt is shredded up to the sleeves and who cares? There isn't any normal flesh to see. My abdomen has opened up and I'm bleeding out. It's a scene from a horror movie. Suddenly I can't feel my back or my pelvis anymore, and a strong chemical smell floods my nose—the asphalt? Truck fumes? The rubber tires that just ripped me apart?

I'm dying.

It feels like thousands of shards of burning glass are embedded in my skin, all over. I'm on fire, but I'm cold on the pavement. Nothing makes sense. My skin is so hot, but my core is cold, and I can't stop shaking. I can see my intestines.

"Why did he do it? Why did he accelerate?" I ask everyone, a question that no one can answer. My mind tries to understand—did he intend to kill me? Did I do something wrong? He looked right in my eyes and then took his foot off the brake and shifted to accelerate.

I came here on a humanitarian mission, to be a peacemaker. Why did someone want to do this? It hurts emotionally as much as it hurts physically. Both types of pain are brutal.

This is going to be it, right here on the pavement. *No! Fight harder.* I can't let myself pass out, or I might never wake up again. All I can think to do at that moment is to keep screaming—my EMT training kicks in and tells me that's what to do to keep myself alert and keep my heart pumping. *Stay in control. Don't go into shock. Stay alive.*

A woman with blond hair appears and sits in the road with me, holding my head. Her breath smells strongly of cigarettes.

"Hang in there. It's going to be okay," she says.

"Please don't let me die! I just found my husband. We haven't even met our child. I can't die now. I can't die!"

"You will make it." She caresses my forehead amid the sounds of tires screeching and yelling all around us. It's chaos. It's chaos and I'm dying. "You will be a mommy. Hold on."

Before long, she is gone, but there are others. Someone is always talking to me, tending to me. Another man runs over, screaming out orders and carrying an emergency heat blanket from a kit he had in his car—he's a retired medic.

"YOU, STOP TRAFFIC. YOU, HOLD HER HEAD STILL. YOU, COVER HER ABDOMEN WITH THIS. Holy...God. Hang in there, girl. Hang in there."

My blood is everywhere. People stop and stare, white-faced. I'm a scene out of a horror movie come to life, and everyone wants a glimpse. Some want so badly to help me live; some are there just to gawk. You could put your fist through the hole in my abdomen.

"Nasty!" one guy says. He is cursing as if I am no longer a person who can hear and feel, but just a spectacle, an object in the road. As if I'm choosing to bleed out here on the pavement, naked, with my open abdomen disgusting as many people as possible. As if I am not trying my hardest not to die at this moment.

Sirens...everywhere. People screaming.

"Call my husband," I manage to choke out to one of the men. I can barely breathe or get a word out, and I keep coughing and gasping. "His name is Sean." I recite the number slowly, barely audible. As the ambulance arrives in record time, this man reaches Sean at work to say that I've been in an accident and that I'm going to the hospital.

"My name is Patti and I'm here to take care of you," the paramedic says.

"Please don't let me die." I say that again and again to anyone who will listen.

"You hold her leg together. You hold this on her abdomen." The EMTs are not there to chitchat. They mean business, and they are moving with speed and purpose. It's a team of three women, and they're rolling my body onto a backboard, just like I learned in training. I was supposed to be one of *them*, not the one being loaded into an ambulance.

I hear Patti say to the young medic, Amanda, "I can't believe she's still conscious."

Lying on the backboard stretches out my open wounds and feels like hell. The pain overwhelms me and I scream, but I picture Sean's face and I fight. If he were here, he would put his hand on my heart and tell me that we're in this together. And that's what I need. I need...

"Would you—put your hand on my heart?" I ask Amanda, who is there to monitor my vital signs. It's her first day on the job. In fact, I am her very first call. I don't know that until later, of course. I just know I am dying and I need help.

"I've just been reconnected with my soul mate," I tell her, every word labored between gasps. "We want to have a baby. I can't die now. Please don't let me die. Please pray that I don't die."

I am pleading for my life, begging total strangers to take control of my destiny. She puts her hand on my heart and promises that I will live. I'm bleeding internally even more than externally and yet I'm still conscious and aware of everything. My training is a blessing and a curse; I know more about what's happening to me than most people would. I know that fecal matter is entering my bloodstream and that I'm quickly becoming toxic. This is one more way I can die.

They pump me full of morphine and Patti tells me, "You should feel a little relief soon. You don't have to fight so hard."

But I can't accept that. I need to fight for my life. I'm woozy and dizzy, and it could be from the morphine, but more likely it's from the trauma and pain and blood loss. To treat an unconscious patient is to work blindly, trying to guess what hurts the most, where the injuries are coming from. I am determined to stay lucid.

My left leg is unresponsive. I can't feel or move it.

They'll amputate it at the hospital, I acknowledge. *Probably both legs. If I live, I won't cycle again.*

It's a terrible thought, but under the circumstances, optimistic. My racing heart strains to pump. The ride to the hospital takes about twenty minutes, and in that time the pain and the fear switch places. The morphine does its job so that the intensity of the pain lessens, but the fear is overwhelming. I may never see Sean again. My EMT Amanda has her hand on my heart and is praying out loud for me, "Dear God, give her grace and strength."

Please, God, let me live.

It's the simplest prayer, over and over, as I feel myself slipping away. I hang on to those last threads of consciousness with every bit of might I have.

We start crossing the Q Bridge to New Haven and the bumpy road surface reawakens my pain.

"We're almost there. Hang in there," calls the driver.

I will. I will. I will.

The ambulance stops. We are at the trauma bay. The double

doors open to the sunlight, and my eyes shift away from the medic's eyes over to the clouds, the bright blue sky overhead. I feel wrapped in love and safe, like I could just float off the table. I am invincible. I am happy. No, I'm beyond happy: I'm suddenly euphoric. I feel so good that I think I could get out of the ambulance and bike another hundred miles. There are hands all around me, reaching, touching, comforting me, and I know I'm all right.

The hands reaching toward me are the last sight I see. My world goes black.

I didn't lose consciousness then, which I know only because of what other people have told me. I have no memory beyond those double doors—but apparently I was cussing up a storm while they were hooking up my IV and assessing my condition. Not exactly the serene state I had been in a few minutes earlier while looking at the clouds. There are stages of death, and I was cycling through them.

Embarrassing, really. Here these people were just trying to save my life and I was swearing and ranting about how the whole state sucked. Shock makes you do weird things.

My chief trauma surgeon, Dr. Kaplan, later told me that the chaplain was holding my hand because they thought I would be a DOA—dead on arrival. They were pretty amazed that I was still not only alert, but coherent and actively belligerent. Still, they knew there was no way that could last. My body was torn apart and I barely had any blood left in it.

"Let go of her hand. She's going to code any second," he told the chaplain—but she refused to let go. She kept praying out loud.

Finally I shut up and flatlined.

"Thank God," said the surgeon. "Let's get to work."

They started CPR and ran fluids through my IV. A trauma nurse ordered more and more blood, running it constantly. The chaplain still wouldn't leave until the doctor screamed at her to "Get out!" because she was in the way. It was chaos. No one knew where to even start on me.

For the next six to eight hours, I kept dying.

I would flatline, someone would do CPR, and they'd pull me back from the abyss again. People had to keep rotating because keeping me alive was exhausting work. At the same time workers were doing CPR, changing bags of blood, and running monitors, the orthopedic trauma surgeon and his team were there debriding my insides—cleaning out the gravel and rocks and debris. My stomach was ripped open, my backside was ripped open, my right iliac crest—the big, elephant-ear-shaped pelvic bone—was severed. The pelvis holds all the vital organs up, so when it's compromised, internal hemorrhaging doesn't stop.

On top of that, my femoral artery was severed. They were trying to clean out all the junk while not causing me to bleed out any further, and I just kept right on dying. The blood would run through me and right out again, over and over. I can't even imagine the mess.

They moved me to a state-of-the-art trauma table that few hospitals had yet. If we were lucky and I lived through the experience, it would help them screw me back together more precisely. But of course, the odds were against my making it through surgery at all. And Sean had no idea.

Chapter 9

Level I Trauma

You don't know me, but your wife has been in an accident. She got hit by a truck and it looks like her leg is broken. She needs you to come to the hospital."

That's what the person on the side of the road told Sean. The man lived nearby and had come out when he heard all the commotion. He was the one who was nearest when I yelled out Sean's number. It was unusual for Sean to pick up the phone when he didn't know the number on caller ID...we were lucky that he decided to answer this time.

"Where are they taking her?" Sean asked.

"Yale New Haven."

"Why are they taking her there? That's an hour away!"

"I don't know, man."

"Is she okay?"

"Sorry, I have to go...the police want to talk to me."

Sean was doing mail deliveries at the time, so he rushed back to the post office to drop off the mail truck, told his manager that he had to leave, and got into his car. He called ahead to the ER, but they had no information on me yet because I was still en route.

So he raced over there, praying all the way, and ran in. When he spotted a police officer working on a computer behind a podium, Sean asked if he knew where I was. The officer didn't, but went to ask the receptionist.

Sean saw her mouth the word "Trauma." That's when he started freaking out.

No wonder they'd taken me to Yale. It was the closest hospital with a Level I trauma center—the level they assign to hospitals that are equipped and staffed to deal with major injuries twenty-four hours a day. In Sean's mind prior to that, a truck had grazed my bike and I had possibly fallen off and broken my leg. It quickly occurred to him that this might be something far worse—but no one was talking. The most he could get out of anyone right away was that I'd been on my bike and collided with a truck. No other details were forthcoming.

"Sir, just wait here and as soon as we find out what's going on with your wife, we'll let you know. Don't worry," the police officer told him.

Don't worry? Did those words ever actually stop anyone from worrying in a situation like this?

Finally, about an hour after Sean arrived, they sent a woman in a business suit out to tell him that I was okay.

"What's wrong?"

"We don't have all the information yet, but I'm going to take you to a family lounge and someone will come talk to you as soon as possible," she said.

"As soon as possible" turned out to be more than another hour.

In between, they kept shuffling him between the family lounge and the more private SICU (Surgical Intensive Care Unit) lounge, because they were sure several times over that they were about to have to send someone to tell him that I had died. The SICU lounge, it turns out, is the place to hear that news.

The next time the woman in the business suit reappeared, Sean realized she was the hospital chaplain. She was there to tell him that the doctors were still working and that I was in good hands, but the more she tried to console him, the more agitated he got. The only thing he figured for certain by then was that whatever had happened, it must have been very bad.

The chief surgeon, Dr. Kaplan, emerged into the hallway for a minute and gave Sean a slightly clearer picture.

"She's on the operating table. I can't say she's okay yet, but right now she's stable. I have to get back in there and monitor her to make sure she stays under control."

"Thank you for taking care of my wife. What happened to her? She got hit by a truck?"

"No, she was run over."

That was beyond Sean's worst thoughts.

Not *hit*, run over. There was a big difference between those two things.

As quickly as Dr. Kaplan had entered, he left again, and Sean was alone to figure out the thousand things that you have to figure out at a time like this. He called my parents to fill them in on the little he knew; by then they lived in Harrisburg, Pennsylvania, and they started driving immediately. He called our landlord to ask him to feed our pets. He let his work know that he wouldn't be in the next day. And he prayed. Over and over, he prayed that I would be okay.

Of course, I was not okay. My heart was barely beating and I was unconscious and split open all over my body. Twelve hours after I left for work that morning, they finally let Sean come in to see me in the ICU. Even as he tried to prepare himself, he couldn't.

The flesh was ripped off my left thigh down past my knee, exposing my bones. Tubes ran into my nose and mouth, and monitors beeped and whirred everywhere. I wore a neck brace. I was bloodied and swollen everywhere, with a belly distended out so far that it looked like I was pregnant with triplets.

We were just starting to try to have a baby, he thought.

Instead, here he was, looking at the incredibly broken body of the woman he'd seen whole earlier that morning. Everything had changed and we would never be able to go back.

Sean gingerly took my cut-up hand in his and tried to send his love through my body. He had been by my side for only a minute when a nurse saw red fluids staining my gown.

"You need to leave. We have to keep working on her now," she said firmly. He kissed my forehead and said a quick prayer before being ushered back to the SICU lounge. He knew from my conversations with him about life as an EMT that you don't mess with hospital personnel—you follow their orders, period. Ask too many questions or show yourself as too demanding and you can expect a lot more silence. Linger too long after they tell you to leave and you won't be invited back in. So he did as he was told and he didn't show anger or insist on more information at any point, even though it was maddening to have no idea what procedures they had done, were about to do, or what my prognosis looked like at that point.

He didn't allow himself to dwell on the idea that I could die, although I'm sure I looked like that was very possible. He fought to remain positive, and hung on every small reassurance the medical team offered afterward—that I was stable, that I had made it through another surgery, that they were just keeping me sedated for pain relief.

At about two a.m., he called Gail in Maine.

"Colleen's been in an accident," he told her. "The doctor said she's going to be okay, but she's pretty banged up. She's had surgeries already and she's intubated."

Gail was too shaken up to drive. Instead, she lay in bed and cried and waited until friends could drive her. My parents, brothers, and sister-in-law were already at the hospital when she arrived, and they told her she could go in and see me in the ICU alone if she wanted to.

Now a paramedic, Gail had seen a lot. But what she saw in that room scared the crap out of her.

Unlike Sean, Gail knew the signs of impending death. She saw how bloated I was all over and how low my blood pressure was. She saw all the bandages, the blood pressure medications, and the machines keeping me alive. She saw all of that…and she said goodbye to me.

Not out loud, of course. But what she saw in me looked just like the last time she saw her uncle before his death. She walked out of that room devastated, believing she would never see me alive again. And she had no idea what to say to Sean, because he was still so optimistic.

He just doesn't understand how bad this is, she thought. *And I'm not going to be the one to break it to him.*

She couldn't make eye contact with him; she just hurried out and said she would be back soon. None of my family knew what Gail knew. She could look at me and see kidney damage, brain damage . . . she had an insider's view that the rest of them didn't, and it was a heavy burden.

Over the next few days, while I remained medically sedated, I was in and out of surgery several times, and not out of the woods by any stretch. Once they had stopped the bleeding and I wasn't going into cardiac arrest anymore, the bigger threat was infection. With all of these huge open wounds, the risk of infection was enormous, and my body wouldn't have the ability to fight back the way a healthy body could.

One time, I woke up just as the surgeon was starting to operate on me. It was absolutely terrifying. I saw a bright light and masked faces hovering over me, and I couldn't breathe. I remember my chest rising and falling, but I couldn't take a breath. As I woke, the pain hit hard, but I couldn't move or communicate no matter how hard I tried. Well, except for my fingers.

"Her fingers are moving," someone in the room said.

"There's no way her fingers could be moving. She's out," someone else said.

I'm right here! I wanted to scream. *I can hear you!* I tried even harder to wiggle my fingers, to move *anything* to let them know that I was awake.

"Maybe she's having a seizure."

Then another masked face appeared right in front of my face, and I remember a strange smell, and then everything went dark again. They wrote down "mild seizure" in my chart.

My father and Sean posted on Facebook to let my friends and family know what was happening, and there was a huge outpouring of love from far and wide. No one wanted to explain just how grave things were, though, so they focused more on the small positives—which mostly amounted to "She's still stable" and "Her body is responding properly to the medications."

There wasn't much else to tell because I was in an induced coma, a life-saving step doctors take to slow down brain function to preserve the brain after a trauma or severe illness, and to bring down swelling to prevent or lessen brain damage.

People have the wrong idea about what a medically induced coma is. They think it means you're totally unconscious, unable to see or hear or respond in any way. But that's not how it actually is. For weeks after the trauma, I felt like I was locked in a nightmare, imprisoned in my body. Sometimes I *was* unconscious, but other times I existed in a state that has no easy comparison—it was my "coma state."

I couldn't focus on anyone or anything, but I could hear sounds and feel sensations. I was so hot all the time that I felt like my body was on fire. All I could think about was how much I wanted a glass of water. I began having thoughts that were almost hallucinations about lying in a pool of water.

Occasionally I would hear a familiar voice, and that brought some measure of comfort. Whenever Sean came into the room, he would call out, "Hey, honey, I'm here." I know that only because he's told me so since then, not because I actually remember it. He says I would open my eyes and look around like I was looking right through him. (Yes, you can even open your eyes in a medical coma.) My brother Erin drove up from Florida in a fury when he got the news, and I had no idea. My parents would talk to me when they came to visit, too, and I'd just stare around the room then, too. I was too out of it to think, *Oh, that's Sean,* or *That's my mom,* but I did sense the familiarity. My fear levels would elevate or drop according to who was in the room. I relished when someone would hold my hand, stroke my head, or comb my hair. That was the only good part.

The dreams were the bad part. Over and over, I had graphic nightmares about being violently raped and sodomized. My only lucid memory of those first couple of weeks after the trauma, even after lots of therapy, is of those nightmares. There was nothing I could do, no way to escape. It felt like one long panic attack and such a horrific intrusion. I had no idea what was actually happening at the time to cause these horrible images, but now I know that they came when the medical staff were doing "wound changes."

My rectum was ripped all the way up to the sacrum, and my vagina was ripped apart, too. The nurses spent hours every day cleaning my wounds and changing the medication and bandages. Even though I was heavily sedated and had a breathing tube down my throat, my blood pressure would spike during wound changes and they would see my face grimacing. Even in that state, I recognized the pain but couldn't process it, so my brain turned it into the only thing that made sense: rape.

That's what a medically induced coma really is like; nothing can take away all the pain without being extremely dangerous. It just makes it confusing and dulled enough so that you don't actually die from the shock of it all. But overmedicating can kill you, too—so they try to sedate you with *just enough* anesthesia to keep your body as strong as possible to protect the vital organs for surgery. Then they also have to add medication to increase blood pressure because the anesthesia drops the blood pressure dangerously low. It's a delicate balance.

So it becomes this otherworldly haze of an experience where your brain tries to put the puzzle together under the influence of heavy drugs. It's not like a trauma-induced coma where you're fully unconscious while your brain resets itself, more like a deep dream state with moments of partial awareness. Other people who've been through it also describe vivid "dreams" where the brain is desperately trying to put together some kind of narrative to explain the foggy signals coming through.

No one had mentioned my probable brain injury to Sean or my family at that point. Miraculously, my face was nearly unscathed and my helmet hadn't cracked, so they didn't worry much about my head. My obvious injuries were all on my lower half, but anytime you have a hard hit like the one I had, you have the likelihood of a concussion and long-term damage. They did determine that there was no internal hemorrhaging in my brain, but they couldn't do cognitive tests on me while I was so out of it, so there was no official determination about how extensive my brain injury might be.

There is so little of that time that I remember clearly. I'm told I was in a lovely corner room with windows, and that my family and Sean decorated the walls with cards and pictures. What I remember mostly was just the sound of the ticking clock.

I learned later that a friend named Susan, who had been a PeaceJam board member, stopped by nearly every day and read poetry to me from a book compiled by Caroline Kennedy. She would later give me the book.

Sean didn't want to leave my room at all. He watched everything that was happening with me and tried to be my advocate. He had to approve surgeries and he watched for any sign that something was wrong. The first time he saw me trying to scream was awful for him. During a wound change, my eyes were screwed shut and my mouth was open in a screaming position, but no sound came out. That's when he knew beyond all doubt that I was in tremendous pain and that I was locked inside my body.

It happened several times a day, and there was little he could do except try to soothe me with his words and his touch—but he took that job very seriously. He refused to leave the hospital for a week, and the staff provided him a cot to camp out in the SICU lounge. After that first week, he headed home for a shower and some fresh clothes, but he found it unbearable to be there. The house was too empty; not only was I in the hospital, still in a coma, but our landlord was taking care of our dog, Sedona, and a neighbor was fostering our cat, Luna.

He cried in the shower and vowed he wouldn't spend a night there until I was home—and he stayed true to his word.

Every night, he slept in that SICU lounge, sometimes with other people around, sometimes alone. He witnessed a few cases where a doctor had to deliver the awful news that a loved one had died. Only then did he understand that that's how close he had come to getting the same news in that same little room.

After another week passed, he realized that we had no money coming in and some pretty significant medical bills about to arrive—so he knew he was going to have to work somehow. Every minute away was stressful, though. Just a week earlier, I was still hemorrhaging internally and doctors had finally located the bleed: One of my arteries was split and the only way to fix it was to insert a titanium coil into the artery to close it off. The coil, which looked like a long, skinny piece of pasta, would stay in my body permanently.

Then there was the fact that I was losing weight, the controversy about whether or not they'd do a tracheotomy (doctors mulled it over, but decided the risk outweighed the benefit), the infections... Every couple of days they would have to cut away dead skin and tissue from my leg, hips, and stomach and rebandage it up to ward off infection.

Things had the potential to radically change from minute to minute, and my family was no longer in town—they had to leave after the first week—so Sean was alone in the hospital with me the vast majority of the time. My parents would come back for a few days at a time, but he had no other support at the hospital. His parents had offered to come help, but he worried it would be too much for them, so he reassured them he was okay.

He wasn't okay. He was terrified for me. I hope you meet Sean one day; he is a bright light and so full of God's love and grace. He radiates joy and love.

By then he knew that there were some serious questions about how I would function, assuming I made it through all of this. I had a colostomy, considering my intestines were still sticking out of my body, and no one knew if it would ever be reversible. I had a feeding tube, a catheter, a ventilator…there was a "wound vac" on my left side from my hip to my knee, which meant that a sponge had been inserted into my giant leg wounds, covered with a film like Saran Wrap, and a tube inserted into the sponge was connected to a vacuum that continually sucked the fluids away from the wound. I had more than three rolls' worth of gauze packing in my abdomen, and countless rolls in my butt.

How long would I need all these things? There was no real timetable; "as long as it takes to heal" was the only response.

On October 29, there was a freak blizzard in Connecticut—a nor'easter that delivered snowflakes the size of silver dollars and forced Halloween to be canceled. Doctors and nurses who were at the hospital were trapped there; no one else could drive in. These people take on a job knowing they're essential workers and can be forced to stay on duty in times of natural disaster and emergencies, even if it means being separated from their families. It's pretty amazing—and I was unaware of all of it, of course. In my world, there was no blizzard. There was just the endless loop of nightmares my mind invented.

During that time, there was some talk of stepping down some of my medications to test my responsiveness—while still keeping me sedated enough for pain management. I was not yet strong enough for the next round of surgeries, and they needed my body to rally because I had a systemic infection.

They began by testing my breathing, turning the respirator on and off over the course of three days to check whether my lungs would take over. After a brief initial failure, it was successful: My oxygen levels stayed perfect, and the breathing tube was removed on October 30, three weeks into my stay. That meant I could no longer be as sedated as I was; the pain medications had to be stepped down to allow my lungs to function properly. This put all future procedures in question because no one was sure how much pain I could handle without the heaviest medications.

It also meant that I would come back to greater consciousness and try to communicate.

It wasn't a cheerful movie-scene moment, though. Not the "Hey! I'm alive!" moment with a big smile that you see in scripted dramas. I was filled with anxiety and dread, not really sure whether I was awake or asleep, or even alive or dead. After a few days of breathing mostly on my own with the assistance of a nasal cannula, I became more aware, though it would be almost five weeks before I returned to full alertness. My first post-trauma memory is of seeing Sean standing by my bedside, talking to me in midsentence. It was so hazy that I had no idea what he was saying, but I knew he was there, and I vaguely remembered being run over. I was in a tremendous amount of pain, and I saw a doctor, so I knew I was in a hospital.

Then I spotted my parents across the room.

I tried to speak to Sean, but my vocal cords had atrophied and my mouth was so dry that no sound would form. I mouthed out the words "When did Mom and Dad get here?"

"They came in for the weekend to see you," he said.

"So quick?"

I thought the crash had just happened and I was amazed that my parents had been able to get there so fast. In my mind, hours had passed. *Maybe* a day.

"Honey, you've been in a coma for almost a month," he said.

That stunned me. I started crying.

"You were run over by a truck," he said gently, unsure whether I remembered. No one knew what I would recall of that day, or of any other day, really. For the next week or two, I would forget the basics pretty often. It was a little bit like *Groundhog Day* for Sean; I'd wake up and not know why I was in a hospital, and Sean would have to remind me again.

As the haze continued to lift a bit, I tried to understand what was happening with my body. Then came the day they finally removed my feeding tube. The nurse said, "Try to cough," and as I did, up came this tube that felt like it was burning a hole through my insides. There were all these unfamiliar feelings—bandages and tubes and monitors all over me. Then I looked down and saw my colostomy bag.

That made me cry harder.

"It's okay," Sean said. "It's going to be okay. Look! When you get that out, we'll have matching colostomy scars!"

He pulled up his shirt to show me, and darned if he wasn't telling the truth…the scar from his snowboarding accident was in the same spot as my incision.

"You said we have Wonder Twin powers…now we have Colostomy Twin powers, too!"

It was a moment of levity in a sea of distress.

In the beginning, I slept the vast majority of the time. I would wake just for a few hours a day, and nurses would crank up my bed to let me sit up a little, do wound changes, ask questions to determine how I was reacting, and try to feed me once the feeding tube was out. I had lost too much weight and I was in desperate need of protein. But my jaw had atrophied, too. Chewing was impossible. I would try and try to chew one bite, and it would hurt and exhaust me and I'd wind up spitting the food out.

So they tried giving me the standard hospital fare for people in my position: Ensure.

I'm not sure if you've ever tasted Ensure. If you have, I'm sorry. If you haven't, I envy you. It's disgusting stuff. Even in my best condition, it would be hard to tolerate, but combined with a ripped-apart digestive tract, it was a disaster. And when you have a colostomy, whatever you put in your mouth very quickly comes right out in plain view, if it makes it that far. Usually I threw up first. Either way, it was nauseating.

"This is so full of junk... corn syrup, artificial flavors, sucralose... can't we do better than this?" Sean asked the nurses. "We want to heal her, not make her sicker. How about we do a protein mix with almond milk and fresh bananas or something like that?"

They had to clear it with a doctor, but soon they agreed. Sean would mix up fresh fruit smoothies for me with protein powder every day. It was so much better in every way—easier on the stomach and so much better for me.

Doctors wanted to start my physical therapy as soon as possible, but they couldn't because my heart was too erratic and my blood pressure spiked too much. In early November, they moved me out of the ICU and into a step-down room where I'd remain for another week, until I was strong enough to go to a rehab facility. Finally, Sean was able to stay in the room with me rather than sleep in the lounge.

When a nurse named Tammy came for a visit in my new step-down room, I put my arms out for a hug. I had no conscious memory of this woman, but something in my soul remembered her.

"Let's take a picture of you two," my dad offered, and Tammy stood beside my bed with her hand on my shoulder. I'm sitting up in bed and smiling in the photo, wearing my nasal cannula. I don't remember the picture at all, or the encounter, but I'm told that there were two nurses in ICU whom I responded really well to even when I was in the coma: Tammy and Toni. When they were on shift and talking to me, my blood pressure and pulse would stabilize. It's amazing to me that even when I was not conscious, I was aware of tender care. I could sense these beautiful people and know that I could trust them—literally with my life.

I was not coherently communicating at this point, although I was trying. I got out some thoughts that made sense, but also talked gibberish at other times. All in whispered tones because I didn't have much of a voice yet.

The nightmares didn't end once I became aware of what was happening to me; if anything, they intensified. I was on edge all the time and couldn't win: When I was awake, I could feel all the pain of the injuries and the wound changes. When I was asleep, my mind flew off into horrific imagery. One night I woke up quietly screaming, and Sean was dead asleep in the recliner next to me.

A male nurse came rushing in.

"What's wrong?" he asked.

I couldn't speak. I was just sobbing. *What's wrong? Pick something. Everything is wrong.*

"Are you in pain? Do you need something for your pain?"

Finally, I squeaked out, "Hug."

He raised his eyebrows for a moment, not accustomed to this request. He put on gloves and ever-so-delicately leaned over and tried to navigate how to hug me without hurting me. Mostly, he just bent over me and I put my arms around his back and patted him and cried. It was very tender. Of course I was in pain, but there are things painkillers can't fix. There is nothing like the psychological first aid of human touch, nothing that's as good at healing the soul.

That was not what I was going to get from MJ, my main nurse practitioner in the step-down room. She was a tall and boisterous woman who wore bright earrings and took no crap from anyone. She dominated the room and was all business, no squishiness. But I liked her, too—she intimidated me like crazy, but I also felt like she knew what she was doing.

"We're trying to get you out of here as soon as possible," she said. "Now let's get you up out of bed so you can be on your way to the rehab facility."

Out of bed sounded like a wonderful place to be, but also a pretty unrealistic place. I was torn apart, stitched up, bandaged, and medicated, and I hadn't used my muscles in over a month. The more I stayed in bed, though, the harder it would be to ever get up. So with my nurses' help, I would sit up in bed and then come to a standing position with my weight on just my right leg, just for two seconds, with nurses holding on to both sides of me using a Hoyer lift—like a crane for human bodies. The nurses would roll me from side to side while placing a heavy canvas sling under my body—imagine videos where you might see a whale or shark get hoisted up and moved onto a boat. Once the sling was under me, they could lift the contraption with me in it high into the air and then swivel me over and lower me into a chair. This way I could sit upright in a setting other than the same hospital bed.

The Hoyer lift hurt immensely. As I tried to get vertical, my body felt heavier than it ever had before—like it was filled with concrete. It took so much out of me that I would have to sleep for hours afterward. I don't remember doing it more than once or twice at Yale before the orthopedic surgeon decided it was too soon for me to be standing, but much of that stay is so blurry in my mind.

One thing I remember clearly is the moment I finally realized the extent of the damage. I had not been lucid enough or strong enough to really look or touch to explore my whole body, until one day I moved my hand over my vagina and felt metal on both sides and in front. I knew I had a catheter, but this was new to me and I yelled out.

A nurse came rushing in.

"Are you okay?" she asked.

"What's this?" I asked the nurse, panic in my voice. "Why do I feel metal all over my vagina?"

"Yeah...your labia were ripped off in the accident. It's a little cosmetically altered, but the surgeon reattached them and they seem to be adhering nicely. The doctor will probably take the staples out next week."

My labia were ripped off. I don't think there's a delicate way to put that, but at a time when everything seemed to be wrong already, this was just a tremendous topper. I tried to take in what that would mean for me, for Sean. For us.

"Will I ever make love with my husband again?" I asked.

"I can't answer that question right now. We don't really know how your body is going to heal."

She was telling me that I might never be sexually active again, for the rest of my life. Maybe my new husband and I had made love for the last time. How do you process something like that?

Coupled with the intense pain, the hideous mess of my body, the flashbacks and nightmares, and the prospect of possibly never walking again, either, I was no longer sure I was glad to have survived.

Six days after I came out of the coma, and after twelve surgeries, everyone was thrilled with the progress I was making. They ordered a walker and a recliner for my room and encouraged me to try to move between the bed and the recliner on my right leg. I had my first taste of solid food: brown rice and vegetables. My wounds were nowhere near healed, but they were progressing the way the nurses said they were supposed to, even if they looked and felt horrifying to me. An X-ray of my pelvis revealed that my bones showed signs of starting to knit. I was meeting the goals to move to rehab faster than expected: I needed to be able to eat a minimal amount of solid food and to stand with assistance, for starters.

Sean remained cheerful. My parents sent out optimistic updates on social media sites so my friends and family could follow along with my progress. My father ended every one with an inspirational Bible verse or a prayer request for Sean and me.

"God is so great," he said.

I wasn't anywhere near that thankful. I felt like a child with all the help I needed just to move, eat, and take care of myself, and I hated it. It became hard to imagine a future free from all of this pain and need. It became hard to imagine a future at all.

That made me feel guilty, too, because all around me was so much gratitude. I asked Sean to write a Facebook post for me.

> I cannot let fear take over my heart. I have to give my soul to God every day. I am so thankful for my family and my friends.
>
> Please pray that God will use this for a reason and that I will be able to manage the pain and the fear. Thank you for all of your love. It's a month later and I'm still at the hospital. Hopefully at the end of this month, I'll be in rehabilitation.
>
> My heart is full of love for everyone.

That's where I tried to focus: the love. It was all around me, from the strangers who had saved my life to the lifelong friends who were checking in with my family every day. It's what kept me going even after I thought I couldn't fight anymore. I was in for a long and agonizing journey, but I was never in it alone.

Chapter 10

Rehab at Gaylord Hospital

AFTER FIVE AND A half weeks at Yale, I was put on a stretcher to be taken to Gaylord Hospital, a long-term care facility in Wallingford, Connecticut. As we neared the doors to go outside, I had a full-blown panic attack. The sounds of cars and the thought of being on the road terrified me. Every time I thought about going outdoors, I saw images of big trucks coming at me. I hated even hearing the sounds of traffic from my window.

During the transfer and the first few days at Gaylord, the distinction between reality and the fuzzy dream state of anesthesia became clearer as I asked my caregivers to continue cutting back on my painkillers. It's not that the pain had actually lessened significantly, but I was afraid of drug addiction and I wanted to stay in control. The haze wasn't a comfort to me. It was maddening. It didn't stop the visions; it just made me less sure of what I was actually experiencing versus what were nightmares.

Even so, I was still desperately tired and weak and spent the vast majority of time lying in bed in my new location, room 111 at Gaylord. Even stranger, the date I moved in was 11/11/11. We decided it was a sign; repeated numbers are reputed to be lucky, or to be a signal that someone is looking out for you. November 11 is also the date my brother Erin met his wife, and they are such examples to me.

My body was working so hard to produce new cells and heal my broken bones that there was little energy left to do anything else. Whenever I moved, I was dizzy. You know how you get a little light-headed when you first get out of bed in the morning? Your spinal fluid needs time to adjust from all that time being horizontal. Now imagine you've been lying down for more than a month. Not only that, but you've been bleeding and losing bodily fluids the entire time, and barely eating. It's like that getting-out-of-bed feeling multiplied by one hundred. I was also prone to passing out. I was still on a heart monitor and blood pressure monitor so the medical team would have a heads-up on when I was crashing.

At least my room was nice. It was a big room with a high ceiling and a giant window. Sean had written a scripture verse on my whiteboard that I looked at every day:

> "Fear not, for I am with you. Be not dismayed,
> for I am your God. I will strengthen you, yes,
> I will help you, yes, I will uphold you with the
> right hand of my righteousness."
>
> —Isaiah 41:10

As cards came in, my family stuck them all over the wall until there was very little blank space left. People made posters and sent pictures, and it was a visual way to remind myself that I was surrounded with love.

My oldest brother, Shawn, and Kaori visited right away, and all I could do was just cry and cry.

"Sis, I guarantee that before you know it, you'll be walking these hallways and being a blessing to other people," Shawn said. "Actually, I would not doubt it if you could come back here and even give a talk after it's all over. You're going to motivate people and be a light. I just know it."

I didn't just know it, but I wanted very much for his words to be true.

In a quiet moment one day, Sean asked, "Do you think you lived through your dream?"

"Maybe I did."

Maybe the recurring dream about dying on a bike had been mental practice, and helped me to know that I had to keep fighting when the real moment came. The mystery of it would stay with me, and I would wonder for some time if there was a message I was supposed to get from it.

My first therapy at Gaylord was occupational. Soon after I got there, a nurse helped me to wash my hair for the first time. She moved me into a well-padded wheelchair and wheeled me into the bathroom and in front of the sink. It was the first time I'd seen myself in a mirror since the trauma, and I hadn't prepared myself for the sight. I knew what I could see when I looked down at my torn-up body, but I'd been told that my face was nearly unscathed, so I hadn't given much thought to what it looked like. Then I made eye contact with myself in the mirror and knew that this vision was real.

My cheeks were sunken in and my eyes were bulging out of their sockets. My teeth looked huge compared to my shriveled mouth. I looked like a skeleton draped in skin. I barely recognized myself...I had aged decades in six weeks. My weight, normally around 130 pounds, was now 105.

Through sobs, I said, "Please put food in me."

"You're gonna be okay, honey," the nurse said. "You've been on a feeding tube for a long time, but we're going to get you fixed up. Let's start with your hair."

She moved me away from the mirror and leaned me over the sink, caringly sudsing up my hair while I tried to make sense of my new reality. I hadn't eaten more than a few bites of food, I hadn't made a bowel movement on my own, I hadn't walked or changed my own clothes in a month and a half...other people and machines had been doing everything for my body, and that was such a vulnerable and scary feeling. I was a person who put a lot of value on my independence; of course this would be horrible for anyone to go through, but being a control freak didn't make things any easier.

The physical pain of the experience was one thing, but the absolute humiliation of it all was in some ways worse. Every day, strangers were seeing my naked, ripped-apart body and having to do the most disgusting, personal things to it. They were shoving packing into giant wounds in my rectum and stomach. They were *lifting up the skin* on my thigh, which you could open like a giant flap, to clean it out and suction out the fluid. They were changing the nasty, ugly, smelly bodily fluids that accumulated all over me: the wound vac, the catheter, the colostomy. Everything leaked. Everything left pools of blood and fluids all over my bed, my gowns, my floor.

My body was a constant source of disgust to me. All the processes that are supposed to happen *inside* the body were happening *outside* mine, and strangers were not only witnessing it but becoming intimately involved with it.

Sean watched every wound change he could and took part as soon as he was allowed; he would have to take over one day anyway, but he wanted to spare me as much humiliation as possible. It was hard to know what was worse at first—either strangers could do this intimate job, or my husband could see me this way. How would he ever look at me romantically again when he had stuffed gauze into a giant, bloody hole in my butt?

He's going to leave me, I thought. He *had* to. There was no way someone could put up with this for the long term and see me as a man is supposed to see his wife ever again. He was so good to me, so devoted, and yet I was convinced it couldn't last.

Every morning when he'd leave for work, sometime between five thirty and seven, depending on his route, he'd kiss me goodbye and tell me, "I love you and I'll see you as soon as I'm done."

Then he'd go, and my mind would wander into terrible daydreams where a woman would stand by her mailbox and wait for him to show up so she could flash him her perfect, unbroken body and jump into his mail truck. In my mind, beautiful women were all over his mail route and he had all day to do whatever he wanted with them. Obviously I wasn't going to get out of bed to check up on him, so it was a perfect opportunity.

He's probably cheating on me right now. I don't blame him.

My heart kept breaking. He'd done nothing to invite my suspicions; it's just that I was so disgusted with me that I couldn't imagine anyone not being just as disgusted. I didn't know who I was anymore. We had been an active couple who ran and cycled together and who made love every night, and now I was an emaciated, sexless, bedridden person with no prospects of ever looking or feeling the same again.

When Sean was at work, I felt totally lost. I frequently rang that call button and asked for someone to come give me a hug.

"What's your goal for today?" one of the nurses asked me one day. I thought she was crazy.

"Well, I can't get out of bed, I can't keep food down, and I'm stuck to a cardiac monitor with electrodes all over my body. What *is* my goal?"

"Then maybe it's just to get through your wound care and get through the day and see that the sun comes up again tomorrow."

She was teaching me something about gratitude even in the midst of my bucket of sorrow. It's not easy to be appreciative when you're in the muck—far easier to do it in retrospect. But setting any kind of small goal and achieving it was something to feel good about. Making it through another round meant I was closer to walking out of the hospital. There's an adjustment that goes along with life-altering events; you have to learn to celebrate everything, even things that sounded ridiculous to celebrate before. Rolling over. Eating a piece of food. A decent sleep. The fact that you woke up that day still breathing.

After about a week at Gaylord, three nurses came to my room to help me up out of my wheelchair and told me it was time for me to try walking.

As they helped me stand, the same concrete feeling returned. It's like my head was a helium balloon and the rest of me was a thousand-pound statue. It took everything I had in me just to move one leg forward. When I did, blood and bodily fluid gushed out of the wound in my backside.

The equivalent of six rolls of gauze was stuffed into that wound, and it was all covered in a plastic wrap, but it didn't matter—I would bleed and ooze right through it all the time. But at least it was usually hidden underneath me when I was sitting or lying in bed. Now I felt the hot liquid flowing out and running down the backs of my legs and then pooling below me.

"Oh!" I said, looking down in white-hot shame.

"That's okay! Don't worry about that!" one of the nurses said. "You just keep walking. You're doing great."

I took just three or four agonizing steps, then I felt too light-headed to continue, and my face went pale. They helped me back into my wheelchair.

It was almost unbearably humiliating, and yet by later that evening, I wanted to try again. I asked them to wrap me up better, so they tried—a nurse patted down all my wounds and then wrapped basically my entire lower body in plastic film. It didn't matter. No matter what they did, I dripped when I walked. My wounds were going to drain all over the floor, and I couldn't bend over to clean up after myself, so I was leaving this trail of disgustingness under me for a nurse to have to wipe up.

I hated myself. For two weeks, I refused to leave my room unless

I was seated with bed pads under me because at least I could keep my fluids contained there—I didn't want to run into anyone in the hallways, where other rehab patients were practicing their walking or being wheeled through.

Meanwhile, the driver who'd hit me was already back at work. His entire punishment at that point was an infraction for failing to stop at a stop sign. Life went on as usual for him, while mine was blown apart.

Wound care and ambulation were my two main tasks in the beginning at Gaylord, and then we added working on motor skills. I had trouble with various tasks, which I assumed was because I'd been in a coma for so long and my brain wasn't communicating well yet; I didn't think much about the fact that I had a brain injury, but that's what it was. My eyes were moving separately; I wouldn't be able to read the clock, for instance, because I couldn't get the muscles of my eyes to move in unison. Then there were other problems with the brain/body signal—I had trouble making my body do the things my brain wanted it to do.

They'd move me to a room with a long table where other people were also working on simple motor tasks. In front of me were my tools for the day, which looked a lot like items from a preschooler's classroom: cards that I was supposed to sort, rings that I was supposed to put together. Then there was a wall with boxes built in that had different-shaped holes—I had to pick up the matching shapes and put them into the right holes, like a toddler's sorting cube.

Around me were two or three other adults in their wheelchairs doing the same sort of things. We were working individually with our own physical therapists, but in the same space. I found it humiliating. It didn't matter that they were all *also* sorting blocks and rings—I just hated that anyone could see me in this compromised state.

There was a ramp in the room where we learned to walk up and down, a bar where we practiced standing, another bar where we improved our balance, and a set of steps to practice on. Then there was the thing that freaked me out every time I looked at it: half of a car, for those of us with car traumas to practice getting comfortable getting in and out of cars again. A lot of my therapy consisted of me pushing my wheelchair over to the car and just trying not to panic while opening the door. In my wheelchair, I was at eye level with the tires and just kept imagining getting run over again.

As time went on, they wanted me to try to walk with a walker. It was so difficult and painful.

"Am I ever going to walk normally again?" I asked.

"We don't know, but we're going to work on it," the therapist said.

They were so damn honest. I just wanted them to say, "Yes! You will walk, and bike, and make love with your husband. Everything is going to be fine in time." But no one could or would say that to me. They never took away my hope, but they never gave me false hope, either. They would put a lot of the responsibility back on me.

"We're in this together," the therapist said. "Are you willing to be committed to this and set a new goal for yourself every day?"

"Yes," I said quietly. Nothing mattered more, even though it would have been a lot more comfortable physically and emotionally to stay in bed.

"We won't know where you're going to end up. All we know is how you're progressing today, and what we're continuing to work on. You'll keep building on your foundation of strength a little every day."

In a way, it was empowering to know that I had some role in my own recovery—it wasn't all up to chance. Some of it was out of anyone's control, but some of it was about my grit and willingness to push through the pain and embarrassment to relearn these simple tasks again. And I was pretty full of grit.

I never got used to the wound cleaning and dressing changes that happened twice a day, every day. Every time I was log-rolled to lie on my side, I knew what was coming and I sobbed and I shook in pain and humiliation. At night, they would wait for Sean to get back from work as often as they could, so that he could be with me. He'd sit on the other side of the bed and hold on to my head and put his other hand on my "good" leg. Then he'd pray out loud while they were fishing around and while I was crying. He was everything at once: a nurse, a psychologist, and my best friend, even as I unfairly distrusted him.

Gail also came to visit again from Maine, and she helped take care of me because of her paramedic training. She admired the all-female team who'd managed to keep me alive in transport and she began talking with them. I mostly just cried through her visit, too.

"This isn't the way it's supposed to be. I'm supposed to be your big sister and take care of you," I'd say.

"Colleen, this is where the tables turn. Now I'm *your* mentor!" she would say.

"I just hate that you're seeing me like this."

Siblings—Shawn age 8, Erin age 5, and me age 2.

Sean's senior prom, Daytona Beach, Florida, 1991.

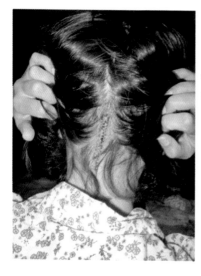

Two weeks post–brain surgery at
Columbia Presbyterian Hospital.

Two weeks post-trauma at Yale
Surgical Intensive Unit, 2011.

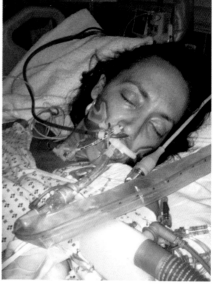

Week 3 at Gaylord Rehabilitation
Center. *(Sean Alexander)*

Superhero Half Marathon
in New Jersey, 2012.
(Sean Alexander)

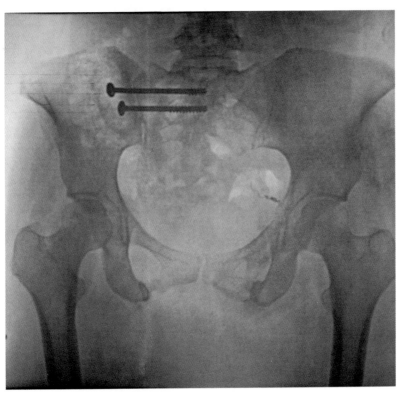

Pelvis x-ray at my two-year post-trauma appointment.

Gasparilla Challenge Race, 2014.
(Sean Alexander)

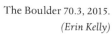

The Boulder 70.3, 2015.
(Erin Kelly)

Newport Marathon,
after surgery 28 to have
expanders implanted,
non–weight bearing.
(Newport Marathon)

David Smith, my hero who was the main witness to the trauma. *(Sean Alexander)*

Runner's World photo shoot. *(Reed Young)*

At dinner in Los Angeles with Archbishop Desmond Tutu after an International Peace Conference.

Madison heroes—Patricia Palaia, Amanda Bernier, and Lyndsay Cummings. *(Adam Coppola)*

Red Cross Gala—my parents, husband, brother, and sister-in-law, with close friends Julia, Brian, Marie, Abigail, and her fiancé, Mark, 2016. *(Red Cross)*

Doing a tree pose in 2016.
(Global Click Photography)

Full circle—honored to guide
Barbara at the Redding Road Race
Half Marathon. *(Sean Alexander)*

Giving thanks at the Red Cross Gala after receiving an award, 2016. *(Sean Alexander)*

Competing in the Atlantic City Triathlon with our nephew Javan Kelly.

An afternoon ride in my hometown, 2017. *(Sean Alexander)*

"I'm a paramedic. I see boobies and butts all day. I meet someone and thirty seconds later, I'm taking their shirt off. You have nothing to worry about with me."

It was beautiful to have her show up, and to have other family and friends show up, too, which they did in large numbers. Neighbors, childhood friends, coworkers, family, all sorts of people would visit to cheer me up. A couple of friends even flew out from across the country. Gaylord didn't have many strict rules about visitors—I could even have friends come chat with me during physical therapy if I wanted.

I liked having people around to hug and hold hands, even though it was also humiliating to be seen the way I was, no matter how anyone tried to be reassuring about it. I was in such a vulnerable position without control over my functions. We'd be in the middle of talking, and then there would be a big fart sound and smell from my colostomy bag, or a gurgling noise from my wound vac. No one really escaped it; if you were coming to see me, you were going to smell poop and hear really gross things. People were cool about it, even if they were inwardly horrified.

Because my eyes wouldn't move in unison, I had a lot of trouble focusing on people and it made me nauseated to keep trying—like a weird seasickness. Sometimes I had to close my eyes and just listen. And sometimes I was so hopped up on Dilaudid that I remembered none of the conversation afterward.

I never felt unloved; there was a lot of support out there for us from the moment I can remember waking up. Most of the time, people just let me cry, and I asked them to pray with me. Human connections were so important. It was gratifying to have people show up whom I had not known well before the trauma, and instantly bond as they looked into my eyes and held my hands and prayed with me.

But one thing several people said started to grate on me: "At least you're alive."

"At least I'm alive"? I'm pooping in a bag, I can't move, I'm in constant pain, I feel like I'm having one long panic attack, my body is torn apart, my husband is sleeping in a recliner instead of next to me in our bed, dozens of strangers have touched my naked body, I'm having unrelenting nightmares... there was no "at least" anything. Every sentence that began with "At least" felt belittling. At least you're conscious; at least the surgery went well. Even worse was "You should feel grateful." "Be grateful you're still here." No, thank you. I couldn't listen to the bright side of anything—it all felt phony. I was just trying to make it through each day, and I did not feel grateful for anything. Especially not for cheery little platitudes.

A housekeeper came in one day to mop and called out as she left, "Hope you feel better!"

Steam came pouring out of my ears. "Hope you feel better" is what you say when someone has the flu. Not when someone's been run over by a freight truck and just got out of a coma. I just wanted people to acknowledge the complete suckiness of the situation, not belittle it with empty words. There was so much that people just didn't understand or acknowledge. I hadn't taken a shower in months. Months. Having a nurse wash my hair once a week (often while I was in bed) was my biggest bliss, but I still couldn't feel the water on my body like I'd always taken for granted. I was limited to careful sponge baths because of my many open wounds. There were so many blatantly ordinary things that I missed so much, and it was hard to see beyond what was happening.

One day they took me back to Yale New Haven Hospital for a follow-up visit with my surgeon, Dr. Kaplan.

"It's good to see you alive!" he said, and I tried to smile. "I wasn't sure if I would get to see you again. You died on me a couple of times."

"I did?"

"Yes. You went into cardiac arrest several times when you first came in. We had someone running back and forth to get you blood over and over."

"How many units of blood did she need?" Sean asked.

He checked the charts.

"Seventy-eight."

"Wow." Sean looked at me. "I had eight after my accident."

The human body holds, on average, ten units of blood at a time. So people had donated the equivalent of about eight entire bodies' supplies to keep me alive. The very idea was humbling, but still, it didn't fully sink in until later.

"You lost so much blood that there was nothing left for your heart to pump. We were doing CPR on you for twenty minutes at one point, but I wouldn't call the time of death. You looked like a fighter to me."

"I had no idea it was that close," Sean said. "All I knew for a long time was that she came in for a broken leg."

I guess it was supposed to make me feel better that I was such a miracle patient. That's what people kept telling me—that it was amazing I had lived at all, much less that I was speaking and breathing on my own and, despite the traumatic brain injury, mostly coherent at this point. *I was such a brave fighter.*

But I lived with high anxiety and depression constantly. Though I didn't have a name for it then, I now know that I also had PTSD: post-traumatic stress disorder, the same condition that affects many service members who've been to war, or people who've been raped or violently attacked. Some of the main symptoms are hypervigilance (being constantly "on the alert" for danger—thinking another bomb is about to drop or another truck is about to run you over), nightmares, flashbacks, intrusive thoughts about the trauma, insomnia or difficulty staying asleep, and having trouble connecting with loved ones. I had all the above. Thank God I didn't know that the driver who ran me over was still making deliveries for the next three years, or I would have never wanted to set foot out of my house.

My family knew I was depressed, but I don't think they knew how depressed. They would tell people publicly that I had "good days and bad days," but the truth is that I never had good days psychologically. Every day was a fight with my brain and agony for my body. Lying in bed was so opposite of who I was that even that in itself was psychological torment for me. I was not supposed to be bedridden; I was supposed to be out there in the world training for marathons, pushing our baby in a jogging stroller, and riding my bike.

"When an athlete gets injured, it's even more of a curse than for a non-athlete," my dad said. "You've been so active that it's even more of a loss to have it taken away." My dad got it. He understood because he had gone through many health ailments of his own and was an incredible athlete.

People sent me beautiful cards and care packages; my dad had given my address out online and encouraged people to reach out to me. He figured it would lift my spirits. Gifts came in every day: a neck warmer, essential oils, lip balm, face lotion, flowers, teddy bears. I was grateful, though I was spiraling so far down that it was difficult to pull out of my funk for more than a few minutes at a time.

A girlfriend made me a beautiful prayer shawl that Sean would tuck around my body when he went to work in the morning. He would also put drops of the essential oils on my pillow or around the room. Nurses would always tell me I had the nicest-smelling room in the place.

Friends would drop off organic juices and kombucha tea, which they knew I loved and used to brew at home. Thank God for that, to counteract the trays of beige hospital food. They'd bring big photos of nature—a strawberry field, my favorite hiking spots—so I could look and stay connected with the outdoors even when I couldn't get out and feel the grass under my feet. Really thoughtful stuff.

PeaceJam sent me a care package that contained candles and fuzzy blue socks. That seemed really nice until I saw the logo on the side: LIFE IS GOOD.

Ugh.

Sean learned that a reporter from *Madison Patch* wanted to do an article about me because Madison was where I was run over, so he coordinated a time with her to come visit Gaylord and speak to my family and me. The reporter's name was Pem McNerney, and I liked her immediately.

After she learned all the details, she asked if there was anything people could do for me.

"I really want prayers and positive energy," I said. "My wounds are huge and it's going to take a long time to heal. I'm trying hard not to get depressed."

"Is there any kind of lesson you want to pass along to readers from this?" she asked.

"It's just that it doesn't matter how careful you are sometimes. Every day is such a huge gift. You have to be ready, vigilant, and aware it could change. No matter how safe and careful you are, things can happen. I'm sitting here in a bed in a rehab facility and I'm scared. I don't know when I'm going to be normal again."

That was about as much positivity as I could muster.

The article went online a day or two later, on November 10, and because of a miscommunication with my dad, it said that I had lost my job after the crash. People were writing angry comments on the article—"How could her employer DO this?!" I wrote a letter to Pem to defend my boss and to assure readers that I hadn't been fired, that I was just taking a break while I was healing. I felt bad that my boss might read these comments and see how people were badmouthing him without cause.

In fact, I couldn't wait to get back to work. I knew I wouldn't be back in the office anytime soon, but I tried to figure out what I could handle from my bed. Sean brought me an iPad so I could write. I updated my blog to let people know that I was alive and improving, and I tried writing to the people whose connections were important at work.

At the very least, I wanted to write thank-you notes to all the donors who had supported the Cycling for Peace trip. My boss had come to visit a couple of times while I was at Yale, and had kept in touch by email since then. I told him that I was going to be back as soon as possible, but every time I asked for addresses or information about the donors for the thank-you cards, he didn't respond.

Just three days after the article came out, I was busy composing more thank-you notes when my boss wrote, "Before you send out any more emails, let me come by."

It wasn't the best day for visitors—I was spiking a fever and they had started an IV again. I was too weak to move much, but I was hoping he might have some good news for me, so I didn't argue. Maybe it was my new contract?

He showed up soon after and had trouble making eye contact with me.

"Can I talk to you for a minute first?" He signaled to Sean to follow him out to the hall. Sean paused.

"You can say whatever you need to say in front of Colleen. We share everything, so anything you tell me, I'm just going to tell her anyway."

My boss sat down next to me.

"Colleen, I'm very sorry to tell you this, but the board is phasing the program out. You no longer have a job."

Chapter 11

Breaking Down

I DIDN'T HEAR ANYTHING CLEARLY after that. I just started sobbing.

This can't happen.

He tried to explain. The board was restructuring in a different region, and he was stepping down, too. It didn't matter. He knew. He had known for a couple of weeks by that point and hadn't told me; in fact he had falsely reassured me, and I had just defended him like a fool. There would be some severance pay, so sorry about this, blah, blah.

All around me were cards and letters from PeaceJam kids. A group in Seattle had sent me a huge paper quilt with inspirational quotes and letters after hearing about my story. My whole life was tied up in this work, with these kids, and now it was the youth center all over again. Blindsided. Not only did I not have a job—and my husband still had just temporary work—but they were shutting the whole thing down for the kids. Again.

They were even using the same stupid word: *restructuring*. That's what they had said about the youth center, and it was bull. No one ever "restructured" anything. They shut it down and they used the money on programs for rich kids. This place was supposed to absolve me of some of the guilt over losing the youth center, and instead I lost both of them.

I can't even tell you how angry I was. How deceived I felt. I had moved here for this, and now as I fought just to regain the ability to walk, I was supposed to figure out my next career move? It was unthinkable. I had no backup plan; this was my calling. And now how in the world was I supposed to pay for my medical care?

I'm sure my boss tried to say something consoling, but I remember none of it. Eventually Sean showed him to the door and told me we would get through this. I couldn't speak. I was devastated, and would remain that way for days. I didn't want to talk to anyone. I just wanted to cry. How was I supposed to tell the kids? I wasn't even sure I would see any of them again. Twice in two years, the programs I had built up were being torn down. This was some kind of magic touch I had.

The more I thought it through, the more I felt personally betrayed. My heart rate shot so high that nurses had to come in to medicate me. Sean was furious. I remember him stomping around and explaining to a nurse what had happened. "We just got her leveled out. She's been improving, and now she's going to need to go back on a heart monitor and everything is going to be screwed up again because of this!"

My days at Gaylord had been pretty consistent after the first week. After Sean left for work, I'd go back to sleep. Then around 7:15 a.m., depending on rounds, the lights in my room would flip on. Someone would take my blood pressure, draw my blood, check my catheter to see if it was clogged or if my urine looked cloudy or crystallized, and check to see if my urethra needed to be flushed out with saline. Then they'd check on my stoma for infection. Everyone would stare at my stoma, the delicate lining of my intestine sticking out through my abdomen to attach to my colostomy bag. Then they'd roll me over onto my side and I'd cry as they pulled the tape off my butt. The wounds in between my butt crack were literally the size of a dinner plate and were closing very slowly.

Often there was someone new: a doctor or nurse who hadn't seen me yet. That's when I'd hear the sharp intake of breath, tongue clucking, or the other sounds of surprise. They'd all seen bad wounds before, but this was nothing ordinary.

They'd eventually move on to my abdomen, which also needed to be cleaned and re-dressed. When I first came out of the coma, that area had felt pretty numb, but now some nerve endings were growing back and it burned more and more. I tried to appreciate the burn because it meant my body was trying to heal, but how much pain can one person take? It was an all-morning pain marathon.

And that's how I woke up every day.

Afterward someone would bring in breakfast. Sometimes I could eat; sometimes I couldn't. They'd set me up in bed and leave me be until the afternoon, when we'd get to do it all over again, usually with Sean.

By this time, I was also having full wound vac changes on my leg on Mondays, Wednesdays, and Fridays in the afternoon, which was the most painful experience of all. The regular RN would come in about twenty-five minutes in advance to give me a strong painkiller and an antianxiety medication, and once I was stoned and groggy enough, the head of wound care would come in and do her thing with her team. They'd start by peeling the wound vac tape off my body from above my hip down to my knee and on my abdomen around to my butt. The tape held on all the plastic "shrink wrap" on my body, and there was Tegaderm, a sealable medical wrap for large wounds, on my leg.

Just getting the tape off was agony because my skin was so raw. It took twenty minutes to peel the tape off each time. Under the plastic wrap was a ton of medical foam. They'd pull that off next and there would be a gush of nasty wound discharge. Then there was another layer with antibacterial ointment that had to be peeled away. All of it had to be changed out frequently to lower the risk of infection. Despite all these efforts, infections would creep in anyway. Just before Thanksgiving, I had an infection in my abdominal wounds that derailed me for days. It started as two separate wounds, but they tunneled into each other and I wasn't able to get out of bed or do any rehab until it cleared up with antibiotics. It looked like a miniature gopher tunnel full of green goo. A week after that, my upper leg wound got infected, too, but at least it cleared quickly.

Once all the layers were off my leg and the wounds were open again, they would pool up with blood. Everything was gross and raw. The nurses would scrub it off with some sort of special sponge while I continued to bleed. This part of the process took close to an hour. Then they'd take big syringes filled with saline and squirt it all over.

"That's good. It's beefy red," the nurse said during one of the early changes. "If a wound is beefy red, that means it's healthy and getting good blood flow. It's when it's not red that it's bad."

I swear, I never want to hear the phrase *beefy red* again in my life. It nauseated me every time one of the nurses said it. I didn't care that it was supposed to be a good thing. Hearing my wounds described the way one might describe hamburger meat was just not cool and felt like even more of an affront because I had not eaten red meat in close to fifteen years. That being said, I adored my nurses. They had become my family, and as horrid and pain-filled as my wound care was, they shared stories, paused for a hug and for me to catch my breath, and many times we even laughed.

After all that was done, it was time to start the process of putting it all back together. They'd lift up my skin and stuff new medical foam in, cutting it to fit the shape of my wounds. Despite the pain medication, it hurt desperately.

Then they'd feed a tube into the foam for the wound vac, put the skin back down, attach the Tegaderm, attach the vacuum hoses, turn the machine on, and check for leaks. More than nine out of ten times, there was a leak. Or leaks. The machine would beep like crazy and they'd have to troubleshoot to figure out where the leak was, because anytime air could get into the wound site, it added to the potential for infection. They needed to have a completely solid seal so bacteria wouldn't grow.

Sometimes they would have to mess around for another hour to find the leak and get the machine to stop its loud, incessant beeping.

By the time the entire process was done, I was exhausted. The cook knew I would need a turkey sandwich afterward. He'd prepare shaved turkey with cheddar cheese on white bread—which was funny because I never liked white bread before—with mayo and a pickle on the side. I would devour it and then sleep for a couple of hours.

One of the reasons I was placed at this facility was that the head of the wound care team was so good at what she did. That didn't stop me from hating the sight of her, of course. Our interactions were not what one would call pleasant. They were torture from beginning to end. One day, I just had *enough*.

When the nurses came in early that morning to check my colostomy and start my wound care after Sean had left for work, I just pleaded for them to leave. I refused to let anyone touch me. I was not going through it again. Not having someone pull my butt cheeks apart one more time to fish around in there. Not going through the agony of being ripped apart from one end to another while holding anyone's hand. Not doing it anymore!

I wanted to die.

I spent several hours crying and bellowing, wishing I had just died on the pavement that day. It would have been finite, not this never-ending battle just to have some semblance of…what? Normalcy? You couldn't even call it that. My life was not going to be normal ever again, and at the moment, I couldn't see it ever becoming even *sort of okay* again. It was going to be eternal torture. And why? Because I took a bike ride home from work on a day when I wasn't even supposed to be working, only to be told the following month that it was all for nothing because I didn't have a job anymore? What kind of ridiculous destiny was this?

I can't even stand up to brush my teeth, I thought. *I have no purpose left anymore.*

I screamed and cried, and screamed and cried some more. Every time someone entered the room I screamed them right back out. I just wanted to be left alone.

Maybe if they left me alone long enough, I would just go ahead and die of my wounds. I would fall asleep and disappear. Maybe that would be better for everyone. Not only was I feeling horrible about the physical effects of my trauma and about losing my job, but I felt so guilty for what it all meant for Sean. Was he supposed to become an abstinent caretaker for the rest of his life? I hated doing that to him, and yet there was no way out I could see. Either he would leave me and I would feel horrible, or he would stay with me and I would feel horrible. Every conclusion I came to was a dead-end street. If I died, he could get remarried without guilt and live a normal life.

And what about my parents? Why did I have to be such a burden on them long after they were done raising kids?

I was so angry about everything. I was mad that God had let me be in that path—and then let me live like this. Was it something I did? *Are You just trying to get my attention? Because this is not the way.*

Then came the guilt about being angry with God. What right did I have to be angry with my Creator?

Why couldn't I have just died?

I lay there in my own waste until one o'clock in the afternoon, steaming mad and sad and guilty and suicidal, wanting to make it all go away with the force of my despair. I was angry with the people who'd saved me, angry with the machines that kept me alive. Meanwhile the nurses would patiently check in on me.

And there, in the midst of all that misery, one thought popped into my mind. It was a quote from one of the PeaceJam Nobel laureates, Jody Williams: "Emotion without action is irrelevant."

I'm being completely selfish.

It hit me that quickly. As I was sitting there moping in my misery, I wasn't doing anything to make it better. Instead I was dragging everyone else down around me when they were just trying to help. I needed to find a path to make this better—if not physically, then at least mentally. The idea of going *poof* in my sleep was not productive; I was a person with worth and value, and I needed to find a new purpose. Considering how much anger I had harnessed, I could use all that energy toward something good instead of something bad.

Screw this, I thought. *I've already been through seizures and brain surgery. Even a freight truck couldn't kill me. There has to be a reason I'm still here. A way for me to become a light in the world again, even if it's not how I expected to do it.*

So I let the nurses do what they needed to do, and then I asked to speak to the hospital's chaplain. He came to my room and read scripture and prayed with me.

"I've been feeling so angry with God, and I know that's not right," I confided. "I know I have no right to question God."

To my surprise, he said, "You *do* have that right, and it's very normal in a situation like this to feel angry with Him. It's okay. God can take it." The Gaylord chaplain was a light, full of God's love. He was honest and full of integrity and I was so grateful to him.

"But there are so many people who have it even worse than I do. There are people right here in the hospital who can't talk, who will never get out of a wheelchair, who have severe brain damage. I know I shouldn't feel sorry for myself when others are suffering worse than I am."

"If you're feeling guilty for not having it as bad as someone else, then acknowledge it for what it is. Maybe you should go to these other people's rooms and talk to them. Try to understand what they're going through. You don't know if there are other people thinking the exact same things as you are—feeling like they can't come talk to you about what they're feeling because you have it worse than they do."

"I don't know what I would say."

"You could say, 'I feel terrible that this has happened to you. This is what happened to me,' and start an open dialogue. Don't be so concerned about tiptoeing around stuff, because they're probably angry, too."

I gave it some thought. The chaplain reminded me of Archbishop Desmond Tutu; he was so kind, so strong, and *always* smiling.

There was a young guy at Gaylord who had been brought to Yale the same week I had. He'd been in an accident in his pickup truck and sustained a spinal cord injury. He was also in the SICU in an induced coma at the same time I was, while doctors tried various surgeries. Sean had gotten to know his mother well during that time, since they were both waiting around a lot. It turned out the young man was a college student and musician.

Sean had told me, "I think you should meet him," so I decided to take him up on it. A day or two after my conversation with the chaplain, I asked Sean to wheel me into the young man's room. His mother greeted us, all smiles.

Sean wheeled me to the side of his bed and I just started crying. I tried to hold his hand, but it was immobile. He was also unable to talk.

The room was decorated with mail from his college friends, and he had an iPad set up in front of him. I wondered what he was doing with it, when his mother said she'd like to show us the music he had been working on before the trauma. She pulled up the program on the iPad.

"He fuses different songs together," she explained. "Now we're going to keep working on it as a team. He shows me with his eyes where he wants me to tap on the keypad."

It was heartbreaking and beautiful that this was how he would continue with his dreams. I wondered if he looked at me and thought that I had better do something good with my life. If that's what he was capable of, as limited as he was, then my avenues were wide open.

"I'm so sorry. I wish I were the one lying in that bed and you were the one here in the wheelchair," I said, like an idiot. I was just saying things before my brain even had time to process what was coming out.

I'm making it worse. Stop talking! What is wrong with me?

Words kept tumbling out anyway, though, and when I finally managed to ground myself to a blubbering halt, his mother gave me a big hug. Then she looked at his eyes and told me, "He wants to play a song for you."

A beautiful instrumental song rang out into the room.

I asked if we could continue to be in touch and visit them again, and his mother said, "Of course."

We would see each other in physical therapy after that, and a few days later, I visited his room again. His mother looked at his eyes and then told me with some excitement, "I think he wants you to know that he can move his finger now."

Sean wheeled me to the other side of the bed so I could see. I wrapped my finger around his and said, "I'm so glad that you can move your finger."

He got to the point where he had some mobility in his arms and legs, but he still didn't speak. Then one day they determined that he had plateaued, so he was discharged. I never got to say goodbye or find out his contact information, and the hospital staff wasn't allowed to tell us.

"If they ever come back, please let them know I'd like to see them again," I told a nurse.

"Will do."

There were moments with other patients, too. We'd meet up in the hallway somewhere because we were each trying to wheel ourselves as far as we could go, and we'd get tired and have to stop. I'd get into random conversations with another person twenty feet in front of me just because we were both there and both fighting that same battle. Soon we were both crying and a nurse would come up behind one of us to say, "You're okay!" and wheel us in the right direction. We'd wave to each other and that would be the end of our moment. But we were each stepping-stones for one another at that point in our lives; sweet temporary relationships based on an undercover code of compassion you'd see in a moment of eye contact or a sad smile.

I became less humiliated about the fact that I still couldn't get all the right blocks in the right holes in physical therapy, and more connected to the other people around me who were also grimacing while trying to figure out their blocks. There was so much unspoken language. *I wonder if this is how babies communicate*, I thought. Just gut-level perceptions, just pure emotion.

Meanwhile, my communities in both Connecticut and Vermont were coming together for me in a big way. One of my youth center kids, Autumn, put together a silent auction fundraiser for me as soon as she heard about the trauma. She would later tell me that she never pictured herself as someone who could organize an event, but that she used the skills I taught her when I organized things for the kids. She and another youth center friend, Val, found a local restaurant willing to host the event for free, and they raised more than $3,000 to help Sean and me with our expenses. My cousin Wayne set up an online fundraising account for friends and family to chip in, too. We used the first of it toward rent, which we'd been unable to pay that month.

Sean's friends had talked to him about finding a lawyer while I was still in the coma. We'd had one meeting with an attorney since I was moved to Gaylord, but I just wasn't able to focus much mental attention on it. Thinking about what had been done to me only brought me deep sadness and panic all over again. It tore away at my sense of humanity to remember that the driver had tried to leave.

My caseworker at Gaylord, Debbie, tirelessly advocated for me and was able to get my COBRA health insurance plan extended for another six months, after which time I could transition to paying for private health insurance. It would be expensive—the private plan would be about $1,800 a month—but an attorney could help me navigate how to get loans to cover my bills for the time being. I would have been in a blind panic if I had known then the magnitude of my expenses to come.

Although we were told that the insurer for the driver's company would have to pay a settlement for what he had done to me, we didn't know how it would eventually shake out—would it cover all of my medical expenses? Would it cover lost income and anything beyond the basics? The process was going to be lengthy and we had no way to predict what to expect. In the meantime, even with health insurance, we understood that the bills were going to be astronomical.

It didn't take long to confirm our fears; the first hospital bill arrived a few days later. It was for just the first three days at Yale: $632,576. Poor insurance company. Poor us.

I tried to focus every day on finding hope wherever I could grasp it. Each day when the nurses cleaned my wounds, they would measure the holes. I began paying attention to what they were saying. One day, they announced that a wound on my hip had closed half a centimeter compared to the week earlier. I started the calculations in my head: *If it took one week to close half a centimeter, then how long will it take to close the whole thing? Let's see... there's a 2.5-inch hole in this section...* and I would begin mapping out my recovery.

Whatever was expected, I wanted to be a healing overachiever. I wanted those wounds closed, and I wanted them closed now. But I tried to focus on a Ralph Waldo Emerson quote I loved: "Adopt the pace of nature: her secret is patience."

On November 23, I took my first step on a mock set of stairs. One step, and it hurt to lift my leg like that, but I did it. As the days went on, I took more and more steps using my walker. When someone told me I would be able to walk across the entire physical therapy room before long, it sounded insurmountable—but then I started being able to envision it. I was my very own Little Engine That Could.

I knew it was unlikely for me to ever get back to where I was before, but I refused to accept that I wasn't ever going to be *me* again. Being an athlete was a big part of who I was. So one way or another, I was still going to be an athlete. Hard to picture at the moment, when I was still dependent on other people to give me sponge baths, but I began focusing on the thought. *Emotion without action is irrelevant. I will get back to who I am someday.*

Toward that end, Sean and the nurses began wheeling me outside when possible. I remember the first time Sean brought me out to the garden, because the light was so bright that it stung—I felt like a vampire. I hadn't seen the sun directly in so long that it was a shocking adjustment. I was intimidated by the feeling and couldn't stay outside too long because I started to panic. I felt exposed. The next time, Sean put sunglasses and a hat on me. It still took a few times before I felt comfortable going out to the garden, even though it was a protected little alcove in the middle of the building complex.

What I really wanted more than anything was to hug my husband again. Not from a lying position or with him bending over to my wheelchair; I wanted to stand up and embrace him fully, with our arms wrapped around each other's backs. I asked the nurses to help me make this happen.

They had to stand behind me to support me and prop the wheelchair against my legs for balance, but we accomplished it. It was the best hug of my lifetime.

On Thanksgiving, Sean brought me down to the conference room to see my family. It hurt immensely to sit on my wound, so I hated being wheeled around—not to mention, I hated having to be so dependent in general—but I was so happy to be with them. I just hoped I would be able to eat something and that I'd withstand sitting down for a decent amount of time with them. When we arrived, my parents, brother Shawn and sister-in-law Kaori, and their two sons were sitting around a beautifully decorated table with a home-cooked dinner.

We prayed together while my wound vac ticked away noisily in the background. It felt so good to be part of a family gathering that wasn't just about my broken body. It felt good to see that my squirmy little nephew hadn't changed, and that my parents could still find reasons to laugh.

I wanted to believe it would be calm seas after that, but of course it wasn't. Healing from trauma almost never is. There would be more infections, though thankfully nothing that got out of control. There would be a day when my colostomy wouldn't stay sealed and Sean would spend two hours with wet gauze and gentle forehead kisses trying to work every piece of tape off my raw wounds so that the nurses could come clean it out and try again.

"Remember, love, we are doing this together, and this is temporal," he said. "You are beautiful."

There would be more times that I would break down and have to remind myself again that it was *not* time to give up. Sometimes my friends had to remind me, too. Mostly, I kept repeating my new mantra to myself about taking action—and one of my first actions was to write a thank-you note to Jody Williams for helping me to turn my thoughts around.

Then, in a flash of inspiration, I hit my call button and asked the nurse to put me through to the hospital's PR department.

"The... PR department?"

"Yes."

"Can I ask why?"

"Because I want to organize a bike tour fundraiser."

"Um... okay."

"I know what you're thinking. But I know how to raise money, and I know how to do a bike tour. I did one for the kids at my youth center and we got seventy-five participants. So can you connect me with the PR department?"

They did. Tara, the vice president of public relations, came to my room. I explained how exercise had always been therapeutic to me, even though I was unable to exercise now.

"I need something to do right now to get out of my depression, and I want to help people find an outlet for their depression and frustration, too," I said. I told her about how much I loved to bike, especially, and how I had read a flyer on the bulletin board about Gaylord's adaptive sports program. I knew that they provided adaptive bikes for athletes with various types of traumas and disabilities, and I hoped to one day be able to ride again. I knew I would be scared out of my mind, but I also knew I had to do it. Biking was healing to me.

With my injuries, I understood I'd probably never ride a normal bike. There were a few people in my life who used adaptive technology, though. A longtime friend of mine had been born missing a bone in her leg and used a prosthetic. She was a serious athlete—a snowboarder and swim instructor. I had learned a lot about adaptive sports from her and knew that people could do amazing things with the right tools and training.

"I'd like to help raise money for the sports program. We can bike along a canal trail and charge people a set fee to participate," I said. "What do you think? Will you help me help others?"

"Of course," she said. "Tell me what you need us to do to support you."

"I don't have the connections here that I had in Vermont. I need you to point me in the direction of people who can help."

That meant media, bike shops, law enforcement to monitor for safety, anyone on the board of trustees for the canal bike trail, possible sponsors for food donations, and so on. I was more than willing to make the phone calls because I didn't have a whole lot else to do, but I wanted a starting point and the credibility of being able to say I was "officially" working with Gaylord on the event.

Even though it was an act of charity, it was not wholly selfless. Every time I had ever helped others, it came back to me tenfold. It's powerful to spend your time in service of others.

Gaylord's adaptive sports program was called the Sports Association of Gaylord Hospital. It's pretty common for rehab hospitals to have programs like this to integrate sports into rehab therapy and to help patients continue to be active after they get back into the community. The program manager came to speak with me about logistics. It turned out that they did have a shortage of bikes because of the cost: Each bike ran about $2,000. I decided my goal would be to raise $8,000—enough to fund four new bikes.

It felt fitting to plan it around the one-year anniversary of my trauma, October 8. That would give me almost ten months to make all the connections I needed to get the event planned and publicized. The only condition I asked was that anyone who had any kind of physical or psychological need to use the bikes could.

Whether or not I would actually participate in the bike tour was a very big question. I hoped that setting it that far in the future allowed for the possibility, but I knew it was still a long shot. Either way, it kept me involved with the world I wanted to be in.

It was wonderful to have something to do again...something to plan and care about. The next time that nurse asked me, "What's your goal for today?" I was going to have an answer. The sun was going to come up again.

Chapter 12

You've Got to Be Kidding Me

YOU HAVE TO LET me go home by Christmas," I begged my case-worker. My depression was mounting; I couldn't listen to patients groan or handle the smells of hospital waste much longer.

"About forty percent of your body is still open wounds. I think that's too soon," she said. They wanted me to stay in the facility at least another month.

"I don't. I need to be home. Sean knows how to do the wound changes and I can have nursing care at home as often as I need it."

"We'll see" was all she would promise.

I had a good feeling about it, though. I knew from what all the doctors and nurses were telling me that I was healing much faster than expected and with few complications. Especially considering that I had an autoimmune disorder and a previous brain surgery, it was truly remarkable, and I was just starting to appreciate it.

Then came the day that my therapist Robyn had promised would happen: In the physical therapy room, she stood behind me holding my wound vac in one hand, my catheter bag in her pocket, and my heart rate monitor in her other pocket, and managed to maintain my wheelchair as my safety net as I slowly inched step by step across the floor with my walker. I could barely look up to see the progress; I was just so focused on not passing out. My back wounds seeped from underneath my dressings onto the floor and my head started to tingle with weakness. Down I went, back into my wheelchair. A blood pressure cuff was quickly wrapped around my arm and I heard a tender voice saying, "You did it, Colleen... It's okay, we got you. You did it... all the way across the room!"

I slept the remainder of the day, with the exception of wound changes, and I dreamed of running. The funny part was that I didn't even like running. I looked at it as a means to an end; I was a cyclist who wanted to do triathlons, so I had to run. But now that I couldn't, I fantasized about it all the time. Someday I was going to run again.

Less than a week before Christmas, I got a terrific surprise: my discharge papers.

The papers listed my diagnosis and follow-up instructions. The space for "primary diagnosis" ran a little long:

- Degloving injury to left thigh from labia majora to left knee
- Multiple pelvic fractures
- Rectal injury

- Sacrospinous injury
- Extensive soft tissue hematoma
- Acute blood loss anemia
- Electrolyte imbalance
- Ventilator-acquired pneumonia
- Metabolic acidosis

It was quite a list, and yet I was standing. Many people on my medical team told me that if I hadn't been a conditioned athlete, my heart would never have withstood the multiple cardiac arrests and surgeries afterward. I had defied the odds.

That day, I stood in front of the bathroom mirror with my walker and brushed my own hair and teeth and looked at myself. I was so excited and scared at the same time. My safety net was disappearing, and I knew I was pushing it to leave so soon. Despite my reservations, I just *had* to be home for Christmas.

Sean helped me put my jacket on and threaded my wound vac through my pants. There was nothing left to be done. It was time.

I had entered the facility on a stretcher; I wanted to walk out. With a walker, of course. Sean took a picture of me beaming while holding on to the sides of that walker for dear life. It was my victory lap. Nurse Lori, one of my favorite nurses and the one who I trusted with the most delicate parts of my recovery because of her patience and compassion, followed behind me with a wheelchair as I made my way out of the room and down the hall. Some of my other nurses lined the hallway with tears in their eyes and applauded as I passed by. How could I ever thank them enough for all they'd done for me? For their expertise, of course, but also for their caring.

I took two breaks on my way to the door, but I made it all the way without needing the wheelchair. It was nighttime. I had asked to leave in the dark because daylight felt too overwhelming. I hadn't been out of a medical facility since the fall; now it was winter, and I was not sure about how I was going to adjust to the stimuli of the outside world. I was terrified of the ride home. I didn't want to be in a car, and more specifically, I didn't want to be near any *other* cars. The thought of having to be on the road with lots of cars around us was terrifying.

Even though I had practiced being around a prop car in the physical therapy department and even worked with the therapists to try to get in and out of a car, you never realize just how difficult it is to get into a car until you can barely sit by yourself in an upright position.

I was heavily medicated with antianxiety and pain pills for the trip, and Lori and Sean helped to get me situated in the passenger seat. I held Lori for a long time and cried and thanked her before she closed the door and sent us on our way.

Despite the medication, I panicked the entire way. It was awful. The vibrations of the car, the smell of exhaust, the sounds of cars passing us—I was triggered up the wazoo and couldn't wait for it to be over. Sean basically didn't stop talking the whole time, trying to distract me.

"Look at the Christmas lights! Wow, look at that house," he said. "I bet that took a long time to put up."

"Mmm," I managed.

He played Christmas music on the radio, too, and tried to keep the mood joyful.

Once we were home, our landlord and a friend helped to get me out of the car and into the house. No Sedona. My enthusiastic dog, who always greeted me at the door, would have to stay with our landlord for the next couple of months while I continued to heal. Our cat, Luna, too, would remain on an extended vacation at a friend's house. It felt so strange and wrong not seeing them as soon as I walked through the door. Sean had hired a professional crew to come in to scrub the house, so when I arrived, everything was fur-free and clean. It felt oddly sterile.

Our friends had cooked my first meal at home, which was there waiting when we arrived. I sat at the dining room table to eat, but then felt the full brunt of being out of a hospital environment: I hadn't sat in a normal chair since the trauma. It was painful. I could sit for only five minutes, and then Sean had to carry me to my wheelchair and put me in bed.

Still, I was home.

Around the bed, presents and mail were piled up. The first thing I opened was a beautiful blue-and-brown hat that a woman named Diane had knit for me. She was a Facebook friend who had become an important resource to Sean because she had also had cryoglobu-linemia and was able to answer his medical questions.

Since my hair was so thin and damaged after the trauma and lack of nutrition, I loved having something pretty to put on. Sean and I took our first selfie at home with it on my head and posted it to Facebook.

As relieved as I was to be back in my own environment, there was also a new reality to consider: If I spiked a fever, if my heart rate got erratic, or if anything else went seriously wrong in my recovery,

I was no longer in a place with a team of people, equipment, and medication ready to deal with it. I would have home health aides every day for the first two weeks, then three to four days a week for wound care (as much as my insurance would allow), but anything beyond their scope meant calling 911 and getting into an ambulance again. I dreaded it. I wanted to believe it would never happen to me, but I knew I still had a long road ahead with several more planned surgeries.

My home health care nurse was a kindhearted woman named Ali. She spent nearly two hours on my dressings every day while I continued to cry out in pain and exhaustion, just as I had in the hospital. Over and over, she told me, "You're strong. God has big plans for you."

On Christmas Eve, my sister-in-law thought it would be good for me to get a little change of scenery. She aired me out a bit by driving us to Starbucks for a green tea latte. I waited in the car while she bought it, vomiting in pain into a barf bag both before and after the latte—which was such a frequent occurrence that it barely registered anymore. Especially after all he'd done for me, I wanted to go to a running store to buy a Christmas gift for Sean, but I wasn't sure I could handle walking in.

"I know how much this means to you. If I find a parking spot right in front of the door, you have to try to come in," she said.

I agreed, figuring the odds were pretty low I'd have to live up to my promise. It was downtown Madison and the street parking was usually very crowded. But sure enough, there was a perfect spot right in front of the door.

We went in together and some of the employees recognized me

from my Cycling for Peace tour. I sure didn't look like a cyclist at the moment, though.

"I got run over," I explained.

As I told them my story, a woman nearby said, "Me too! Well, not run over, but hit, and I read all about you! I was hit by a UPS truck a few years ago. I don't think my injuries were as extensive as yours, but it still took a huge toll on me. I want to give you a Christmas gift…"

I wondered what she was talking about, and then she walked down the aisle, picked up a book, and came back to pay for it. Then she handed it to me. It was *The Long Run: A New York City Firefighter's Triumphant Comeback from Crash Victim to Elite Athlete* by Matt Long.

"His courage to survive helped save my life," she told me. "I hope it will do the same for you."

We both cried. I started reading it in the car. Matt was an athletic New York City firefighter who had been run over by a shuttle bus when he was on his bike one day. Like me, he'd had a very slim chance of survival and had needed significant blood transfusions. Like me, he had questioned why he survived. But he had gone on to train and become an Ironman triathlete once again, and was dedicating his life to inspiring others to overcome their great challenges.

One of the central themes of his message was "No longer will I wish…no longer will I want…from now on…*I will.*"

My new friend in the store was right; it was just the right message at just the right time, and she reminded me how easy it was to become an everyday hero with a kind gesture. Her sense of empathy led her to give a gift to a complete stranger just in the hopes of being helpful, and it worked. It was a shot of inspiration to read that someone had been through something so similar to what I'd gone through and had come out on the other side *that* strong, and that confident, despite his scars. I wondered if I could do the same.

My family came in to Connecticut that day. Erin was not able to be there because of work, but on Christmas, we got him on Skype on the iPad so we could still take a full "family portrait." It was an awesome day. I wasn't as active as I would have liked to have been—I kept having to sleep on and off throughout the day—but it was just so good to be surrounded by people and my home and my things rather than beeping machines.

It really wasn't until after Christmas that the "new normal" set in. I was finally back in my home, but it didn't make me magically me again. I was like an entirely different person in an entirely different environment. Navigating everyday tasks that I used to take for granted was a challenge; I longed to do even the normal chores like laundry and dishes, but I couldn't stand up for long or lift things. It might have been nice to get out of housework for a while if not for the reason for it all—I hated that there were things I could not do, while knowing how lucky I was to have loved ones all around me ready to take over everything that needed to be done.

Constant reminders of what I was missing popped up all around me; friends of mine would post their pictures of New Year's Eve dance parties and I was stuck in a recliner on pain medication as I wondered if I could keep my eyes open to watch the ball drop on television. The next day, while they were enjoying days off from work and taking road trips, I was enduring four grueling hours of wound care. It seemed a pretty depressing start to a new year.

"It's okay. You know you have a few tough months to go, but you're going to get through this," Sean reminded me.

"Promise?"

"You're the strongest person I know. Of course I promise."

Every now and then I'd regain a skill, though, or do something that had previously been impossible. On January 14, 2012, I walked up a beach ramp with my friend Erin Christiansen without using my walker, just holding on to the guardrails. That was so exciting that I did it twice more just for fun. Later that day I took my own shoes off for the first time post-trauma by using a reach-it stick. I learned to take nothing for granted. I was *delighted* to take my shoes off!

It's wondrous how many things you can find to be thankful for when you look for them. Just the act of noticing all the things you can do and how many gifts you have in your everyday life can ease stress and improve your outlook. My life seemed to overflow with both—sources of stress and things to be grateful for, often overlapping.

Now that I was out of a job and medical bills were starting to give me heart palpitations, we took out high-interest loans through our lawyer's contacts so that we could survive, but Sean felt a lot of pressure to bring in as much money as he could. He began working lots of double shifts and taking on side work as a personal trainer. But I was really never alone—either my family was there or my friends were. I had a team of everyday heroes: people who took time away from their own needs so they could attend to mine.

My girlfriends set up a calendar so they could each sign up for shifts. Those who lived nearby might tag-team every few hours, while people from out of state would come in for a few days at a time to take care of me because there was still so little I could do for myself. One friend drove up from DC, several friends from Vermont, Kaori from Pennsylvania...they would overlap to make sure that I was nearly never in the house by myself. That was good for both my physical and mental well-being. I was still working through a lot of anxiety and depression. It helped to reflect on my grandmother's words of wisdom: "If at the end of your life, you can count five friends who've been with you the better part of your life, you are lucky." My life had almost ended—did that count?—and I had a lot more than five friends who were showing up for me in a big way. If getting squished by a truck was good for one thing, it was the ability it gave me to see dear friends whom I hadn't seen in years.

It also seemed I had some friends I'd never even spoken with before: the nurses who'd cared for me while I was in a coma.

After I had an MRI at Yale one day in January, my mom asked if I wanted to visit the ICU.

"Sure," I said. I wondered how it would feel to see the place months later. A nurse led me to the room that had been mine. But when I walked through the doors, I felt...nothing. I had no memory of it at all. I had spent an entire month of my life there and yet I drew a blank when I tried to "see" myself there. Probably a good thing that I had blanked so much of it out, but I did wish I remembered the nurses, many of whom greeted me with tears in their eyes and big hugs.

It was so good to be able to say thank you to them. These were people who had helped me in my most vulnerable times, and I hoped I could convey to them what they had given me.

Thank you for keeping me alive. Thank you for the fact that I'm here to go out to lunch with my mom. Thank you for the fact that my husband will kiss me good night tonight.

At the end of January, we went to visit my cat, Luna. It was a six- or seven-mile ride to Guilford, where she was staying. The ride there went pretty well. The ride back did not.

We were on Boston Post Road approaching the same intersection where my crash took place when a woman driving a car blew the stop sign and started making a turn from Neck Road, looking in the opposite direction, and front-ended us. I went berserk.

Police arrived within minutes and issued the driver a ticket. She would drive away with nothing more than a fine, and I would be stuck in a living nightmare. Frozen in fear, I didn't want to get out of the car so it could be taken out of the crash scene and safely off the road. Although I was physically unharmed, I was deeply mired in a panic attack, convinced the world was out to get us. Maybe I *was* supposed to die in the first wreck, and this was a follow-up attempt.

The same newspapers and network news programs that had covered my trauma now dashed out new stories: LOCAL WOMAN GETS HIT AGAIN AT SAME INTERSECTION! It almost sounded like a conspiracy theory.

I didn't want to get back in a car again after that, but on Valentine's Day a couple weeks later, Sean wanted to take me out on our first "real date" since the trauma. How could I resist that? I wasn't in good shape yet, but I thought it was important to try. We went to a small restaurant that was just at the top of our block, and we headed out early so it wouldn't be crowded with the dinner rush and it wouldn't be dark outside. I took ample pain medication ahead of time so I could handle sitting in a booth, which I managed to do for about an hour. It was great. I clung to those little bits of okayness— *Look at us, here, doing what normal people do.*

When dinner was over, Sean said, "You're doing so well. Why don't we try to walk around T.J.Maxx and get you a pair of shoes?"

It was nearby, and I had my walker with me. I was pumped about the idea because it meant I would get a lot of exercise. *And* a new pair of shoes.

Sean drove us to the T.J.Maxx parking lot and helped me get out of the car and situated with my walker. Then he went back to the driver's side to retrieve his wallet. I took my little-old-lady steps to the back of the car with my walker, my wound vac slung across my neck, and I had made it just to the trunk when the guy who was parked next to us in a brand-new Mercedes threw his car into reverse.

He had been waiting for his wife to get out of the store, and as soon as he spotted her, he cut the car around to turn to get her. All I could see was this car coming right at me with its engine revved up, and I screamed.

I tried to run with my walker, but my body wasn't put together enough for it. I could barely take baby steps, yet my brain was telling me to *move faster*! I threw myself to the ground over my walker to get out of the way, and my wound vac burst open.

SLAM! Sean pounded his fist on the back of the guy's car to get him to stop. The driver rolled down his window and yelled, "Don't touch my car!"

"Are you kidding me? You almost just ran over my wife!" Sean yelled.

"She should have been looking where she was going!"

"She's got a walker! She was just run over four months ago! You can't see her?"

"Not my problem if she's not paying attention. I didn't do anything wrong."

Sean called the police, but I was too worked up to answer any questions.

"Just get her to the hospital ASAP," he said to the police officer.

An ambulance arrived, and I was so shaken up I could barely speak. I had to be lifted up off the ground and onto a board again, buckled onto a stretcher, whisked away by ambulance like on the day of my trauma, and examined in the emergency room. Luckily, it was just a matter of getting my wound vac reattached; I had no significant new injuries from the fall.

But I didn't want to leave the house after that. In my mind, the world had become a completely unsafe place. To make it worse, we tried to file a report so that the driver would be responsible for the cost of my ambulance ride and ER bill, but the police said the parking lot was "private property" and they wouldn't get involved. The driver never so much as apologized.

Was it the state that was cursed? Or just me? The thought of it broke my heart. I felt so defeated in my attempts at reentering the world. I wondered if it was time to just give up.

Chapter 13

We All Bleed Red

THREE DAYS LATER, I got a mysterious call on the home phone.

"Is this Colleen?" a woman asked.

"Yes."

"I've been collecting all the newspaper articles about you. I have a stack of them in my living room, and I've always intended to call you. I live about an hour south of you in Milford, and I'm a cyclist, too. It's been heavy on my heart to call you today, so I finally decided to do it. I want you to know that everything that's happening to you is happening for a reason."

I had no idea who this woman was—maybe just a random crazy lady—but at that moment, this lady was the voice of reason I needed to hear. I felt like I was absolutely falling apart and the world had gone crazy; I was ready to latch on to any bit of encouragement I could find.

"I'm guessing you want to leave the state," she said.

Tears streamed down my face. "Yes," I said. "I hate it here. I hate everything about it. I'm terrified to leave my recliner in fear that something else is going to happen to me. I think there's a very negative presence that's literally out to get me."

Maybe it was because I'd gone through two divorces, or because I'd stopped attending church regularly. Maybe God was punishing me.

Very matter-of-factly, she said, "Colleen, I've been reading about you. You have quite a story even before your trauma. You moved here to do peace work and advocate for others. People who are doing strong work of peace and love will never have it easy. You are meant to be here. Every bit of negative energy in the world is trying to push you away and make you quit. Don't let it."

We spoke for about five minutes. She told me that the area of town where I had been hit was also the site of witch trials, which very few people knew anymore. It seemed to be a haunted place.

"This is not the time to fall victim to self-pity and judgment, but rather to rise up and know that you are being picked to go through this, to persevere and be a light. Swords aren't forged in snow; they're forged in fire."

I never heard from this woman again, but she changed my life. I don't know how she knew that I needed her call that day, but her voice reminded me that there were so many people out there pulling for me...people I'd never met before. I took her call as a connection from God.

What I thought about, more than anything, was all the people who had saved my life. I had become a product of heroes.

My brother Erin had been my first hero when he rescued me from drowning. On the day of my trauma, there was David Smith, who witnessed the crash and came running to my rescue. I was covered in blood and he did not react in fear and leave me. Responders were present and they called 911; they called Sean; they stopped the driver; they kept me talking.

Then there were the three EMTs who raced out and capably tended to me so I'd have a fighting chance when I got to the hospital. Then there were all the doctors, nurses, anesthesiologists, and other medical staffers who literally brought me back from death more than once.

And there were the staff members at the rehab hospital who helped me walk again and relearn basic tasks, and cared about me enough to believe in my success.

But what I kept coming back to was one group of people I had never laid eyes on: the strangers who had donated blood that kept me from dying on the surgeon's table.

In order for me to receive those 78 units of blood, as well as 25 bags of plasma and platelets, more than 180 people had to donate theirs. What I began processing was how amazing it was that I now had a little bit of all those different people inside me.

I had no way of knowing how many men, how many women... how old they were, what race or religion they were, what their sexualities were, whether they were rich or poor, whether they had donated blood a hundred times before or this was their first time. I began picturing this group of people and what I saw in my mind was beautiful.

I saw a world united.

I saw black, white, and brown, of all different ages and backgrounds. In my mind, I saw an amazing group of diverse people all conspiring to help a fellow human whom they'd never know, for no reason other than to save a stranger's life.

We all bleed red. It was a statement that encapsulated this journey. As someone who had grown up being a bit afraid of anyone different from me, it now felt like a giant hug from God to realize that I had at the very least 180 people's blood flowing through my veins, pumping through my heart.

How could the world be against me when 180 people did this for me?

That day was a major turning point in my psyche. I would continue to have plenty of bad days in terms of my physical health and pain levels, but that phone call and all the thoughts it set off chipped away significantly at my depression, which had felt like a boulder on my chest until then.

I repeated it to myself over and over: *The world is not out to get me. There is so much love here.* I saw it in my neighbors, who continued to show up and help whenever we needed anything. I saw it in my family and friends. I saw it in my landlord, who offered to put our rent on hold until we could pay it back. (It was such a generous offer. We eventually paid it back in full.) I told myself to *pay attention!* There were good people everywhere.

Gratitude swelled in my heart. How would I ever say thank you to all of these people? I could, and did, say it in person to the heroes I knew about, but there were so many more I would not even recognize if we were standing next to each other. Strangers who had pulled together to save another stranger, just because.

And that's when I started feeling the exact opposite of cursed: I felt blessed.

I didn't know yet what God wanted me to do or learn from my trauma, but I knew my survival had not been an accident. He had put so many wonderful people in my path not only to keep me alive, but to keep me *living*.

I had a husband who had slept by my side every single night, whether I was conscious or not, whether he had to sleep in a seated position or in a cot surrounded by strangers. A man who was now in charge of cleaning my wounds and helping me with every little task and yet never once looked at me with anything other than complete love. Little by little, my unfounded fears had fallen away. This was not a man who would ever abandon me; he never seemed to tire of his caregiver role, and showed no resentment at all for the ways our physical romance had to be put on hold indefinitely.

Just before the trauma we had been planning on having a baby and doing triathlons; now we were staving off infections and watching my body make poop. I had to let go of my shame about it all, and to trust that whatever was meant to be was going to be.

Like before, that Jody Williams quote felt so useful: "Emotion without action is irrelevant."

My feelings of gratitude needed to morph into action.

I continued working to plan the cycling tour, and Tara from Gaylord regularly came to my house to help organize it. Our first order of business had been to identify safe and secure routes, and then we needed to get permission from each of the towns we were cycling through. We opted to cycle the Farmington Canal Heritage Trail, formerly a canal and then a railroad path until floods damaged the line in the 1980s and it was reimagined into an eighty-four-mile recreational trail.

Once we had that set, I started working with the public relations department to secure sponsorships for T-shirts, arrange for police presence, figure out food and drink, get insurance for the riders and the organization, and, of course, start selling tickets. A lot of preparation goes into an event of this size, and it was good to have something positive to focus on.

Around the same time, I had to go back to Yale to prepare for the first of my new round of surgeries. This operation was for the removal of a six-inch bone that had broken off and calcified by the right part of my labia. It meant more anesthesia and some potential side effects, but it also probably meant that it would be more comfortable for me to move around without a jagged corn-cob-textured bone poking my innards.

As Sean and I left my appointment, we passed a room with a sign on the door that said RED CROSS BLOOD DRIVE. I opened the door and saw Yale employees in scrubs lying there having their blood drawn—everyone from nurses to doctors and secretaries. I stepped into the room with my walker and I just crumpled in tears.

Someone asked, "Are you okay? Can I help you?"

"These are the people who saved my life," I said.

I started rambling about who I was and what had happened. Someone who was helping to run the blood drive called out, "Was your trauma October eighth?"

"Yes," I said.

"I never met you, but I remember running blood to the hospital that day. I was at the Farmington headquarters and I got a call saying there was an extreme need for blood at Yale because of a severe trauma."

There were so many people I had imagined in my mind as saving my life that day, but one person I had never pictured was the driver who was transporting blood. I hadn't imagined the people who process and filter blood donations, either. There were even more people on my team than I had realized.

"I was working that day, too," another worker said.

"Me too," someone else added.

I made a mental note of it all: donors, phlebotomists, volunteers, coordinators, the people who package the blood and transport it to headquarters, people who process the blood, people who take the blood where it is needed...there was an amazing collaboration of workers and volunteers to allow this life force to be supplied to someone like me who would have died without it. All these wonderful people rolling up their sleeves selflessly anchored me back to my love of the Red Cross and what it does to save lives.

It reminded me of how important my work with that organization had been. People pay a small amount of money to get certified in CPR, first aid, or other important training, and they walk out with the ability to save someone. They get a new superpower. Little had I known that one day I would need CPR myself. I had also been a longtime blood donor, never expecting that in the future both my husband and I would be on the other end of the equation.

I ended up staying in that room for an hour and a half, hugging people and taking pictures with them. It was soul-affirming. Once again, I recognized these people for who they were.

I am the product of heroes, I said to myself, and it was real. This was what it meant to be part of the human family—to take some discomfort and give your time and a piece of yourself without ever knowing who would get it on the other side. Whether they'd look like you or nothing like you. Whether their beliefs would match yours or be diametrically different.

Afterward I got a call from the Farmington Red Cross headquarters, asking me if I'd be willing to be more involved with their public relations. Would I? Of course! I promised to find ways to speak about blood donations and the Red Cross whenever possible, and to participate in efforts to improve numbers at local blood drives.

To that end, I began making that a qualifier whenever people in the media asked for interviews: They had to agree to mention the need for blood donations. I was very lucky that so many local people cared enough to want to see updates on my story, which meant that news teams from all the networks wanted to interview Sean and me every couple of months. NBC, ABC, FOX, WFSB. I realized I could use this for a greater purpose by making sure they allowed me to speak about causes that were important to me. Finally, I began to see the usefulness of a platform like this. I might not feel glamorous going on television with my stringy hair and colostomy bag, but I could do some good by getting airtime for the Red Cross.

In March, my cousin's wife gave me a flattering new chin-length haircut—I didn't know it was possible to salvage something fashionable with so little to work with!—and I started seeing the difference in my weight. I had gained back twenty pounds since October, and along with looking better, I also started feeling a little better.

"Want to do another Green Up Day cleanup this year?" Sean asked me.

"Of course!" I said with a laugh. "I can use my reach-it stick to pick up trash."

"You're a pro with that thing now. It'll probably be very efficient."

You know what? It wasn't. But still, I was out there with my walker and my dog and my husband and my neighbors and my grabby stick and it was *fun*.

"Hey, what do you think about doing the Branford Road Race this year?" I asked Sean. It was a race we had run together the previous June.

"What do you mean?" he asked.

"Well, obviously I'm not going to run it. But they do allow walkers."

"It's five miles. I just don't want to see you overdo it before you're ready."

"I won't. Well, I probably won't. But if I'm feeling up to it, don't you think it's a great idea? It would get so much press and I can wear a Red Cross shirt and turn it into a blood drive event."

"I've learned never to doubt you."

It was with that blind optimism that I decided to register both of us for the event. As I expected, it drew a lot of attention. The race would be just eight months after my trauma, and looking back now, it was kind of insane to sign up for something like that when I was still dependent on my walker to make it to the end of my block. But it gave me something to strive for.

By the end of the month, I wondered if I'd made a mistake.

I had to go back for another major surgery to reattach my sphincter and close some tunnels that weren't closing up on their own. Basically, doctors were re-creating my butt. I had to have it done if

I ever wanted to have my colostomy reversed...*which I 100 percent did because seriously now.*

For two months ahead of the sphincter surgery, I had intense physical therapy to prepare for it. Once the surgery was done in April, I would not be allowed to bend or lift anything for up to eight weeks—which was also the amount of time before the Branford race. Until then, I would have to shuffle-walk without lifting my legs more than a couple of inches, or I'd risk breaking open my stitches and compromising what the surgeon had done. The strangest part was preparing me for how to get in and out of bed. Imagine trying to get in and out of bed without bending at the waist or lifting your legs up.

The physical therapist, Matt, put rails on the sides of my bed and then taught me to go through a series of movements involving my arm muscles: plank down the wall, plank down onto the bedrail, then plank onto the bed, and from there, Sean would lift my legs up and pivot me onto the mattress. The same sort of rules would apply to getting me in and out of the car—I couldn't sit down, so the car seat had to be adjusted all the way into a near-flat position and I had to plank my way in and out using only my arms. I didn't suspect I was going to do a lot of riding around in a car, but there would be surgical follow-ups, and you just never know. At least my arm muscles were stronger than they'd ever been by the end of our sessions.

"Now...what if you fall?" he asked me.

"I have no idea?"

"Okay, get down on the ground with me and let's figure this out."

He taught me how to crawl up the wall to get myself standing again without bending or curling my body. It was humiliating, but I knew it was useful. He also made it clear to me that I was going to need twenty-four-hour help for those eight weeks because there was little I could do for myself. All I was really allowed to do was shuffle gingerly from place to place.

Although I was never casual about surgeries, I figured I'd been through the worst of it already and this would be more of a speed bump. The day before the surgery, I went to a PeaceJam conference and spoke to a packed room about what I'd gone through, thanking the students and mentors for all they'd done to encourage and support me.

Northern Ireland's Nobel Peace laureate Betty Williams gave me a hug and told me, "The bells of Ireland sounded while you were critical, and the local churches prayed for your recovery."

All the way in Ireland, prayers were being lifted in my name. What a heartwarming thought.

Because of my cryoglobulinemia, the surgical team had to take extra steps during surgery prep to warm up all the fluids and equipment and make sure warm air was blowing on me at all times so that my blood wouldn't clump up with proteins. Then it was time for me to gather up my courage to say goodbye to my husband and tell him I'd see him as soon as I awoke.

A friend had sent me a silver stone with the word *Faith* on it that I brought to the OR with me, and I tried to visualize what it was going to be like to be in the recovery room afterward, drowsy and sucking on ice chips. What a relief it would be.

Except that it wasn't a relief at all. The next few days were the worst of my entire recovery. During the surgery, I had been strapped into an upside-down V position on the adjustable OR table, butt up. So my butt was the high point, and my head and legs were down below during the entire lengthy surgery. Heavy straps kept my legs and chest in place, and medical tape pried my butt cheeks open while the surgeon worked. The goal was to re-create all my sphincter muscles and anchor them to my sacrum. The pain was the worst out of all of my surgeries. Positively horrid.

When I woke up, I had a lot of trouble staying mentally okay. Not only did the area of the surgery hurt like crazy, but I also had bruising all over my chest and legs from the straps. I didn't even fight the idea of painkillers this time—I was on a morphine pump that delivered medicine to me every six minutes. I had a coccyx wound drain tube sticking out of my backside like a tail, and I was kind of *wishing* for that coma again.

This time, I couldn't see visitors except for Sean. I didn't even want to talk to anyone. It was an awful pain in the ass—literally. And I was back in the land of IVs and catheters and antibiotics and nausea all over again. To top it off, we wouldn't know whether the surgery was a "success" for some time. The goal was continence: The only way I could ever get rid of my colostomy was if I was able to use the bathroom normally again (or at least semi-normally). The doctors couldn't just pull the colostomy out to check, so they were going to have to do a series of tests over the next few months to see if my nerves were reawakening.

So at least for the short term, there was no real payoff to this surgery. It just meant more pain, more bleeding, more dependence on everyone around me to take care of me like a child again, with the hope that I'd be thankful later, when I might get to do *another* surgery to close up my stoma—the piece of my intestine that stuck out of my body to deliver waste into the bag. Or not. There was a significant chance I was going to need a colostomy for the rest of my life. Just as I'd finally hit a pretty stable patch in my recovery, this blew it to bits. I had almost forgotten how miserable I could feel.

Luckily, as soon as I was released, the same group of girlfriends showed up for me this time as well.

My friend Maire greeted me at my door one day carrying a butt-shaped cake that she'd brought all the way from a bakery in DC. I'm pretty certain it's the first time the baker had an order to create a butt cake with a Band-Aid over it and this sentiment written in icing:

> *I hope your recovery is a blast*
> *Now enjoy your piece of ass*

An online friend posted a beautiful photo of a rock she was holding against the backdrop of a mountain, with a Navajo prayer for my healing that she'd inscribed into it. It was very serious and beautiful...until you realized the rock was also butt-shaped.

Really, what would I do without friends?

As the days went by, I thought more and more about the day of my trauma and what had happened to my physical belongings. My cycling shoes had broken away and been ripped from my feet, which was a very positive thing, because if they had not, they could have caught on the wheels and dragged me farther. I wrote to the shoe company to thank them for creating shoes that had worked this way. My beloved bike was obviously a mangled mess, and the seat pole had impaled me, but I just wanted to see her again. The police had it as evidence for the impending court case against the driver's company, but I wondered if they could just send me a photograph—so I asked.

What I received gave me goose bumps. They sent a photo of my bike with an evidence tag hanging from the warped spokes, among dozens of boxes of case files on industrial shelves, like a broken old friend. The hood, fork, wheels, and seat would all need to be changed, but the frame was still usable. I was going to rebuild her someday. Just like we were rebuilding me.

The police chief also returned my pannier, which at the time had contained fifteen thank-you cards addressed to the fifteen people who had housed us on my Cycling for Peace tour. All those cards frozen in time. I assumed my hosts would understand why they'd never reached their destination.

A few weeks later, the shoe company, Specialized, sent me a pair of top-of-the-line cycling shoes that cost more than anything I had ever put on my feet, to replace the ones that had ripped off. Along with the shoes came a note encouraging me to ride again. It could not have been more special when Cinderella got her glass slippers. These were mine. Sean even slipped them on my feet for me to check the fit, and it was perfect. They were gorgeous and luxurious, and although I was nowhere near healthy enough to get on a bike yet, they just made me want to all the more. Like a little jolt of energy to get you going on your path. I continued holding out hope that I'd be ready to ride in time for the bike fundraiser in October. People were already signing up for it as soon as we advertised it on Active.com, but I had no idea if I'd actually ride or just cheer people on from the sidelines.

Spring rolled around, which was usually my time to garden. Since I wouldn't be able to get down and dig in the dirt this year, Sean improvised. He created two wood mini-steps right out of the sliding glass doors of our bedroom because I couldn't take the big step down to the deck anymore, and then just past the door, he put up a shelved greenhouse filled with rows of vegetable seed plantings.

If that's not love, I don't know what is.

He had such an enormous smile on his face when he showed me his work, and I was overwhelmed with love once again. This guy cared for me beyond reason or measure, and I just wanted to be the kind of wife who deserved him. I wanted to be out there planting with him and training together, taking spontaneous trips and snuggling up in bed without any weird tubes or stitches to care about. Setting aside the guilt was difficult, but I had to remind myself that who I was right now was enough.

In my dreams, I still ran and biked. In my waking hours, I struggled to walk around the house. But I kept moving forward in my mind anyway—planning for the next thing, and the next.

We should get a pipe-and-drum band for the Gaylord cycling tour, I thought. *And for the after-party the next day.* Of course we would have an after-party!

Being stuck in the house all day at least yields some time for creative thought. And baking. I did lots of baking. I would toddle my walker right over to the counter and cook all day just to have an activity to do.

On May 1, my surgeon finally gave me the green light to sit again.

"Just don't go all crazy and jump into a chair or try to hop on your bike and do a fifty-mile ride," Dr. Reddy said. Pfft. You'd almost think he was reading my mind. *Today, sitting. Tomorrow, biking to New Orleans.*

For thirty-six days I had not sat down without a special cushion, and I mostly had to lie down or stand up. But on May 1, I did some of the best sitting of my life. I couldn't wait for Sean to come home so I could show him how well I could sit!

"Notice anything different about me?" I'd say.

"Your hair? Your lip gloss?" he'd reply.

"No. My butt in this totally normal chair made for normal humans."

It didn't get old the next day, either. I SAT in the car. I SAT in the chief trauma surgeon's waiting room. I wanted to show off and sit on his table, too, but convention dictated that I was probably supposed to lie down for the exam. But there would be more sitting afterward, with selfies! Don't get me wrong: It was still painful to sit, but at least it was progress.

Riding this high made it a little difficult to hear what Dr. Reddy was telling me: that this was going to be a two-year recovery period. I was starting to have fantasies about running or cycling on one of my bikes again in the near future, but he forbade it.

"You can walk all you want, though," he said.

Well, that was...something. Kind of anticlimactic, but at least one limit was being lifted. I was allowed to go outside and walk as far as my legs wanted to take me, and so I did. I started walking with a partner until I tired myself out every day. I wasn't training so I could win a race or beat any personal best scores anymore. I wasn't training for speed at all; now I was training for my next surgery.

Doctors had consistently told me that the reason I had lived and healed so well to begin with was because I was an athlete, but now it had been months since I had done anything more active than walk down my block. How would I continue to heal if my greatest weapon was gone? I had at least six more planned surgeries to go, which meant a lot of anesthesia and new incisions. My body was going to be in the best shape it could be for each of those surgeries, even if I was fairly limited to walking and upper body exercises like push-ups, since the holes in my abdomen were just closing.

So now I was training with a whole new purpose in mind, one that allowed me to see past the disappointment of not being a competitive athlete anymore. In my heart I was still a real athlete, just not someone who would set records anytime soon.

May turned out to be a big month for me in other ways. I volunteered at a bike and pedestrian fair in town to encourage people to bike or walk to school and work, where I connected with lots of local cyclists and bike safety activists. It was a soul-affirming day, and I learned about plans to complete the Shoreline Greenway Trail so that people would have a safe place to commute to work, play, and get exercise. Thinking about the idea of commuting without any cars sharing the space all the way from East Haven to Madison made me giddy. I would never have been run over.

The next week, I got on an adaptive recumbent trike for the first time, with Gail and the specialists from Gaylord's adaptive sports clinic by my side. Amazingly, I was able to use the same Giro helmet and glasses that I was wearing when I was hit—the only evidence that anything had gone awry was a few scratches on the helmet. It had proven itself to be a very capable brain bucket, so I decided to keep it as a lucky charm—though I now know that once a bike helmet is in a crash, it should never be worn again. I was also wearing my new orange jersey that said DON'T RUN ME OVER with a helpful illustration on the back.

My bike was low to the ground and they positioned my pelvis upward, with my upper body leaning back comfortably. The adaptive sports program ran out of pedal bikes, so Gail had to use a handcycle version—a bike you pedal with your arms instead of your legs.

Only a few rotations into it, I felt the natural high of being on a bike out in nature on the Farmington Canal Heritage Trail. Surely it wasn't the same as before, but oh! It was still wonderful.

"Isn't this great?" I said to Gail every five seconds throughout the ride.

"Yeah, I guess," she said. "Whatever makes you happy." Her arms were killing her with the handcycle, but she kept her mouth shut about it because she hadn't seen me so elated about anything since the trauma. Even though it might be a long time before I could get on a "real" bike again, this satisfied my need in a way I hadn't expected it would.

I thought of all the times I had biked or run past disabled athletes when I was in a race. I didn't give them more than a passing thought in most cases. Riding on trails wasn't high on my favorites list back then, either—I would have thought it was too slow and boring. Now here I was, one of *those* athletes riding *that* trail, and it was so freeing that I never wanted it to end.

It was on those trails that I met people from the Achilles Track Club, now called Achilles International. Dick Traum, the first amputee to finish the New York City Marathon, started the club in 1983 to encourage other people with disabilities to run. He formed a group of disabled athletes and able-bodied volunteers to support their efforts in training and running races, and we had a branch right here in my hometown. It was joyful to meet others who were on the same path as I was, and I happily joined the club.

I got so high from the experience that I decided to do the next crazy thing: the Superhero Half Marathon in New Jersey, in which everyone dresses as superheroes.

About ten months after the trauma, I started out at 7:15 a.m. with my trusty walker and crossed the finish line in happy tears at 11:50, kind of jog-walking (don't tell my physical therapist). Talk about a rush! I had no idea if I was going to be able to walk that far, and I had to stop at mile 5 to empty my colostomy bag in the back of an ambulance, but I accomplished it while wearing a Wonder Woman costume with a cape. How does life get better? I'll tell you: It doesn't.

Afterward, I gave my race T-shirt to my physical therapist because without him, I never would have been as far in my recovery as I was.

The next day I went for my next surgery, which was the really exciting one: to get rid of my colostomy. For ten months, a piece of my intestine had been sticking out of a hole where it attached to a bag, sort of like a detour for my digestive tract while my body healed. But now, the bag, the hole, and even the piece of intestine would go away. I wrote it a little goodbye note:

Dearest "Little Buddy,"

I can't really lie...I haven't dug getting to know you that much over the last ten months. I am sorry your home got wrecked from my seat post after that stupid freight truck ran us over.

You certainly were good at making friends. I tried to keep you quiet in public places, but you were stubborn and always seemed to want to "chime in" at inopportune times to let people know you were sticking out of my stomach. We also had some bonding moments, like when I ignored you and ate all that kale and hot peppers anyway...you told me you would be angry, but I had to learn. Regardless, your home has been remodeled since October. I think you will find your newly improved accommodations quite comfortable and hope you settle in nicely. I'm not too sure I'll miss you, but if I do, I know you'll still talk to me, only your voice will exit through the proper end, so I can dismiss myself and we can have a conversation in private. Please don't give the surgeons a hard time, just go back into your home without arguments. I promise, it will be OK. Hopefully we will never ever see each other again, but know I am always right here with you.

Sincerely,
Colleen, your landlord

P.S. You have approximately one more hour to state your piece, so get it all out of your system. T minus 60 minutes until lockdown.

Really, it was all fun and games until they took the darn piece of my intestine out and closed up the hole, and then holy potatoes, was it painful. Dr. Reddy had to put my intestines back together, remove five inches of abdominal scar tissue, and repair two hernias.

I was back to pacing the floors two days later, though, and had the most unexpected celebration: I farted and the nurses applauded. Go, intestines, go.

Many of the people around me were recovering from cancer-related surgeries, and I met women of extraordinary beauty and strength as we shuffled around together, some hanging on to IV poles. Every one of us had a story and a reason to fight. All different, yet all the same. We all bleed red.

Before I was discharged, the attending physician examined me. He looked at my abdominal wound and the way it was healing and said, "Beautiful."

Beautiful?

My first instinct was to say, *No, my stomach used to be beautiful. I had a six-pack! It was a great stomach. Now it's a mess of wounds and scars, and it kind of looks like I got run over by a freight truck, because I did.*

But then I just sat there for a few moments watching that abdomen rise and fall with my breaths. I felt the gurgling and creaking of a reawakened digestive tract. I saw the miraculous way my body had closed up gaping holes. And I thought, *I'm alive. He's right. This is beautiful.*

Chapter 14

Stillness and Motion

Upon arriving back home, I was shocked by the news that I'd been turned down for Social Security disability benefits.

The letter said, "Although your condition is severe, we expect it to improve. While it is clear you will be unable to perform work you have done in the past, you can perform work that is less demanding. We have determined your condition is not expected to remain severe enough for twelve months in a row to keep you from a full-time job."

I wondered how many of them had experienced being run over by a truck.

Even if I had felt capable of finding a new job at that point, can you imagine who would have hired me in my condition?

"Hi! Yes, I understand I'm hobbling around with a walker, but the good

news is that I'm pooping on my own now. Oh, and also, I have at least five more major surgeries coming up in the next year and a half, and in between, I may not be able to walk at all. I'm told I'll need a wheelchair and a home health aide after some of those surgeries, so you'll need to know that I won't be able to come into work for at least a couple of weeks each time. I also tend to throw up a lot and I have panic attacks, and I'm not cleared to drive for five more months. Have I showed you my wound vacuum yet?"

"You're hired! Start tomorrow?"

"Great! I can be there right after my home health care nurse finishes my wound care."

It was depressing to not even be able to contribute a government-sponsored check to my household. If my trauma wasn't good enough to qualify for a year of disability, whose was?

By then I had nicknamed my wonderful home health care nurse "Angel Ali." She had a soft, sweet voice and beautiful clear blue eyes, and was made for the nursing profession—she was so professional and respectful in the way she provided care, but also so nurturing that I felt like she was my sister.

I knew all about her twin sons and her daughter, all about her Irish family and her background. And I learned about her animals: chickens, ducks, and partridges. She spoke about her chickens with such affection, as if they were all her children.

It was the way I'd always felt about Sedona, who had come home in March, but who just seemed so lost now. The day she came back, she couldn't seem to get a handle on what was going on and why I smelled different and moved so awkwardly. She was blind by then, and all the newness confused her. Now there was a walker, a cane, medical supplies, bedrails. It broke my heart to see her so unsettled, and I thought she would get used to it—but she didn't.

I longed to care for her the way I used to, but neither one of us was in good shape anymore. I was a broken-down person and she was an old, blind dog. It was unbearable that I couldn't fix what ailed her.

Ali could see that I needed something to care for. One day she told me, "I just had a few Silkie chicken eggs hatch and wondered if you might want two of them once they're old enough to be on their own."

"What are Silkie chickens?" I asked.

"Hang on, I'll show you."

She pulled up photos on her phone of these crazy-looking chickens with white furry-type feathers, a fluffy pom-pom of feathers atop their heads, black faces, and huge five-toed purple feet. They looked like Dr. Seuss characters, and I couldn't stop laughing. How could I not want them?

When the time came for us to adopt them, she brought two young Silkies out and we were immediately in love. They were so much fun! They loved to follow us around the yard and garden. Sean could literally run along the shoreline and the chickens would run after him, staying right at his heels. Before long, we had five little chickens of different varieties and a big coop on the back deck. Having these adorable creatures nesting in my hands and peeping away at my feet was a form of therapy.

I also started cognitive behavioral therapy around that time to work through my psychological trauma. Since I couldn't drive, I hoped to find someone who would see me at home—even though

I knew that was going to be a huge hurdle. It breaks a therapist/ client boundary that's not normally crossed. But given the circumstances, I hoped someone would be willing to come to me until I was stronger and able to drive myself.

I also knew what type of therapist I was looking for, considering I'd taken psychology courses and seen therapists before. I didn't want someone who would just parrot back the things I said and then ask, "So how did that make you *feeeeel?*" And I didn't want someone overly analytical who would tie everything I was going through to something missing from my childhood. I wanted someone who would be willing to get down in the muck with me and truly help me get through all the depression, anxiety, anger, and doubt I felt, both now and about all the things I knew I would experience in the future: more surgeries, getting behind the wheel of a car again, a civil trial against the driver's company, inability to have sex, inability to have a baby.

I found Leslie Hyman through a friend's referral, and felt a connection with her right away. She showed up at my house and said exactly the right thing: "I'm here to help you as you go through this hell." In fact, that's what she would say to start every session, though I didn't know that yet.

I sat in my big recliner, the place in the house I gravitated to the most because it was well-cushioned, adjustable, and made of leather—so it could be easily cleaned when fluids seeped out. It was my go-to spot; I could recline all the way back and fall asleep, or sit upright to do physical therapy arm and leg exercises.

Leslie didn't seem determined to "fix" me or label me with a diagnosis, which I appreciated. She was good at just being in the mess with me, meeting me where I was in my recovery and helping me cope.

"I'm just so anxious," I would tell her. "I'm forgetful, I'm jumpy... I don't feel like I have a handle on any of it, and I don't think I'm doing a good job of moving forward."

"It's okay to not be okay," she said.

It took a minute for that to sink in. It was a simple statement, but profound. I was pressuring myself to hurry up and get better, but she taught me not to rush it. I had reasons to be anxious, and angry, and every other feeling that had cropped up. It was all normal and fine to own those feelings and sit with them rather than trying to get rid of them right away.

"It's just that I don't know what to do with it all sometimes. This man who looked right at me and ran me over...he's never made any effort to apologize to me or check on how I'm doing. I know nothing about him, but I wonder about him all the time. How he could do it. If he ever thinks about me. If he regrets."

"You should write him a letter."

"I couldn't. I wouldn't even know where..."

"You should write him a letter and *not send it*."

Well, that made more sense. And so I did. Over and over, I wrote to this man and told him everything that had happened to me— all the things I was once able to do that I couldn't anymore, all the things that were lost to me forever because of the bad decision he made. I asked him what his life was like and why he had kept driving.

I wanted to believe there was something other than evil behind that decision, so I focused on fear. I imagined he must have panicked in that instant and I tried to believe that there was some explanation for why he was so scared beyond just the selfish fear of getting caught. In Connecticut, the penalties for hitting a cyclist were disturbingly light—literally a fine of ninety dollars for failing to exercise "due care" in avoiding a collision. Cycling associations had been fighting for tougher penalties for years, but even as of 2017, nothing has passed. So it couldn't have been that, could it? He wouldn't have risked letting me die on the pavement to save ninety dollars, right?

The more I thought about it, the angrier I felt, and I didn't want to feel that way. I searched my heart for all the grace I could find. I wanted so badly to forgive this man, but I had nothing to base it on.

I channeled some of that energy into activism, speaking out in the media about the need for safer roads and stronger laws. I began paying more attention to the news reports of other bike traumas, which came in with alarming frequency. An organizer with the group Ghost Bikes also reached out to me; they attached white spray-painted bikes to street signs near where fatalities or serious bike crashes had happened, along with plaques to memorialize cyclists who'd lost their lives. It was heartbreaking to fully realize what a large problem this was. What had once been something that happens to "other people" now felt deeply personal to me; cyclists were out there getting paralyzed and killed on the roads every day, and our legislators seemed to be ignoring it.

Of course, it wasn't all the motorists' fault. I wasn't blind to the fact that many cyclists pay little attention to bike safety laws. Some ignore stop signs, some weave too far into traffic, some don't wear helmets. The job of respect is a two-way street.

Sean got angry when he saw a cyclist riding against traffic one day. "If people are going to be on the roads, they should have to take a safety course."

"You mean like passing a road test to drive a car?"

"Yes! When you buy a bike, you should have to take a class before you can ride on public streets."

I figured it would never work from a legal perspective, but the thought was solid. There's a reason cyclists get a bad reputation for being entitled and irresponsible. Because of my dad and his bike shop, bike safety was drilled into my head from the time I was a toddler on my first three-wheeler. Not everyone has learned even the basics of bike safety, though, or realized that the same laws that apply to cars also apply to them—no biking the wrong way down a one-way street, for instance.

But the people who drove me the craziest were the ones who should definitely have known better. I was completely distressed when one of my own surgeons revealed that, while he cycled to and from work every day, he didn't wear a helmet! Even after what had happened to me. I realized what I had to do: I brought him my helmet. The one that had saved me from having my skull cracked open on the pavement. I'd thought it would be with me for a long time, but now it needed a new home. Though he couldn't wear it, I trusted that my doctor would appreciate the symbolism.

I didn't want to let legislators off the hook so easily, either, so Sean and I did whatever we could to support the efforts of bike safety groups in our area, by being both volunteers and mouthpieces in the media.

My doctors kept telling me to relax and let my body heal, and I kept responding, "Are you kidding? Have you *met* me?" Relaxing was not a skill I was good at. My whole life, I was someone who was constantly in motion, physically and mentally. I didn't *do* downtime. And for the first months of my recovery, it was something I fought against and frankly hated—I wanted to be back at work, back at training, back at my normal fast-paced life. But something wonderful happened to me that spring: I learned the art of stillness.

Not all the time, mind you. I still had things to do. But for the first time I can remember, I found myself sitting there in my garden with my new chickens, my cat, and my blind old dog, sipping my coffee, and just being. Not doing. Without struggle. I read a letter from my pen pal—my grandfather's sister, who exchanged handwritten letters through the mail with me each week from Pennsylvania—and I wrote back in my neatest script.

I transplanted some peppers, and then the mood struck me to just lie down in the grass and listen to the sounds of nature: the birds, the wind in the trees. I felt the sunshine on my face and I felt...happy.

It was so weird!

Soon after that, it was my nurse's time to say a professional goodbye. She had been telling me for months, "Someday you won't need me anymore, and I can see us just being friends," but that day sneaked up on me. After five and a half months, her last visit for wound care arrived in June, and I was discharged from home health care. It was bittersweet.

"You're strong enough. You and Sean are an excellent team and you can manage your wounds on your own now," she told me.

We both teared up a bit. I smiled and said, "Well, I guess we can just be friends now."

I had grown so accustomed to our sessions together; we talked about everything there is to say. I believe that sometimes, God does put people in your path who are meant to be with you, and Ali was one of those people.

I would soon get the great pleasure of seeing three more of those special people: my EMTs, Patti, Amanda, and Lindsay. First I got to speak with Patti, the paramedic, on the phone. Then I went to the ambulance service to meet with her and Amanda in person.

That's when I learned that I had been Amanda's very first call. She was a part-time EMT on nights and weekends, while Patti was a full-time paramedic and part-time transporter.

"You were one of the worst calls I've ever seen since I've been on the Madison squad," Patti said. "And the worst one that lived. We could see your hip bones, your pelvis, your intestines, tire marks across your abdomen...but you just kept praying and fighting the whole ride."

Patti had tried to come visit me at Yale, but wasn't allowed to due to privacy rules. Seeing them now, hugging them, made me giddy. I wanted them to see how far I'd come. I had just recently transitioned to using a cane most of the time—going back to a walker only for long or challenging walks. And as long as I was fully clothed, you couldn't tell that anything was wrong with me. What was underneath, of course, was another story, but people really had no idea unless I wore shorts or showed my abdomen.

After that day, I went to visit my EMTs every few weeks and often brought them Starbucks or food.

My friend Gail told me that was a funny thing.

"You're saying thank you a lot."

"They saved my life. How could I not?"

"It's just that we're the behind-the-scenes people, usually. It's really unusual to have somebody come back to say thank you."

"Well, that's just sad."

I was connected to those three women in ways that felt permanent. It was Amanda's eyes I was looking into when I thought I was experiencing my last moments on Earth. It was her compassion I felt in that terrifying time. I could not have been in better hands, and I just wanted to thank her every day.

I know what it feels like to be appreciated and I know what it feels like to *not* be appreciated. I made a conscious effort to verbalize my gratitude to people because I know how much it can positively affect the recipient.

On one of my first visits, I told the EMTs, "I'm doing the Branford Road Race next week." They stared at me in astonishment. "Well, I mean, I'm not running. But I'm going to wog."

"Wog?"

"Walk-jog."

I had made it my mission to get the blood banks filled up by the time I finished the race. There were two local blood drives that day, and I made a big social media push to get people to sign up to commit to donate blood in the days leading up to the race. Since I had needed seventy-eight units of blood and twenty-five bags of platelets and plasma, my goal was to get enough people to donate to at least cover that amount.

NBC came out to film me for a series of commercials for the Red Cross, encouraging people to donate blood. They wanted people to see my face—to humanize the idea of blood donations so that it wasn't just a clinical experience. They sent a film crew to my back-yard to interview me, and the chickens and Sedona made special guest appearances.

"Without those more than one hundred people who gave of their time and their blood, I wouldn't be here," I said in one of the com-mercials. "When you sign up to donate blood, you'll know that I'm someone who benefited directly."

I was booked on five local radio shows to talk about it, and there were several new articles about me that week to mark the historic occasion of our return to the Branford race. On June 17, once again I had to use a walker, and Sean wrapped my wounds with extra gauze and taped me up tight to avoid leakage.

My trusty iPod and headphones always came along with me, too. Hearing the sound of my heart beating fast set off panic attacks—it reminded me too much of the fact that I'd gone into cardiac arrest, and it made me paranoid that my heart was going to give out on me. I didn't like hearing or feeling my heart thump . . . or noticing that it was too still, either. I'd lain in bed for so long watching and listening to my heart monitors, knowing that changes in either di-rection would send nurses dashing in. In short, my heart freaked me out. So I drowned out the sounds as much as possible with alterna-tive rock—in particular, "Dare You to Move" by Switchfoot, which had a special meaning to me . . . we had played it at our wedding, but now it took on a different gravity.

I wore a Team Red Cross T-shirt and my race number, 708, and headed out to the starting line early that morning. Sean ran the race, too, but he actually *ran* it. Finishing in just over forty-five min-utes, he headed back to find me along the race course and didn't see me anywhere. For a few minutes, he panicked, thinking I might have had a problem and had to leave the course. He started asking people, "I'm looking for my wife. Have you seen a woman with a walker?"

People laughed. They thought he was playing a joke.

Really, though, I was just farther along the course than he expected I could have been. Despite that I was definitely not supposed to be jogging, I was pushing my wogging to the max. It just felt so good! I finished that race and I got the best news afterward: There had been record-breaking numbers at both blood donation sites. We'd done it; we'd replenished that blood supply, at least for that day.

I had just learned that June and July were the months blood donations were most needed. People who usually donate blood go on vacation in the summertime; schools don't host their usual drives; in short, it's a time when few people are thinking about donating blood, so banks often have a shortage. It felt good to help fix that problem.

The natural high of all that exercise kept me going for another couple of hours, but then it caught up with me: I got home and just *crashed*. That was going to become an ongoing theme for me: I loved taking part in races despite how improbable it looked, and it always took a lot out of me because my body was still deep in healing.

"Can I swim now?" I asked my doctor one day.

"Yeah, sure, as soon as you find a sterile pool!" he said.

"How about a saltwater pool?"

"No way."

"Well, that's no fun. How am I supposed to be a triathlete again if I can't swim?"

I'm not sure which of us was more exasperated. He explained that my skin was still in a very compromised state and would be for quite some time, if not forever—I was always going to be more prone to infection than other people, and considering what my body was already going through, a simple infection could turn into something much worse. No pools for a few more months at minimum.

But at least I had my three-wheeler bike to use, and I was positive that one day I was going to get on a regular bike again. In fact, when I wrote to the bike company Jamis to ask them about potentially sponsoring the cycling tour I was organizing for the adaptive sports program at Gaylord, I also told them about my trauma and my beloved bike—and along with agreeing to become sponsors, they sent me a commuter bike. With my new cycling shoes and my new bike, well, now I was practically *obligated* to ride again. That would convince my doctor, wouldn't it?

Chapter 15

Light Peeks In

Summer was a time of healing and renewal. We grew an amazing bounty of vegetables from seed in our greenhouse and garden: carrots, tomatoes, squash, peas, broccoli, kale, chard, edamame, spinach—all kinds of good, healing food courtesy of the earth. We ate greens two or three times a day. And we found good people to share them with, too, like our local dentist.

He had read about my trauma in the newspapers and also noted that I had lost my job. So he called Sean to offer a free cleaning and exam. When it turned out that Sean had cavities, he did the fillings for free, too.

Good people are everywhere.

I looked for ways to channel my interests and abilities into some kind of "hobbyist income," even though I knew I wasn't ready for a regular job yet. I learned how to create body scrubs and natural lip balms tinted with minerals. I began making prints of my nature photos, and a friend of mine who owned a gift shop offered to carry them for me. She even had me display my "artist photo" and bio on the sale table, and I would work there occasionally selling my wares.

I started volunteering at blood drives, too. One day, just after someone had introduced me as a "spokesperson for the Red Cross," a woman who was waiting to give blood lifted her eyes and looked straight into mine.

"You're Colleen," she said.

"Yes."

"I saw you in the commercial. That's how I knew you were still with us."

Her eyes brimmed with tears as she explained that she was also a cyclist who had been riding her bike on October 8, until she hit a portion of the road that was closed off and she couldn't go any farther. She didn't know what to do, and got into conversation with people nearby. Rumors swirled about a bad accident and possible fatality.

When, finally, she was allowed to ride through, fire trucks and police cars were still on the scene, and the freight truck was still parked with my mangled bike underneath.

"I saw the pool of blood where your body lay, and I just stopped, cried, and prayed. It was all I could do," she said.

We held hands and cried together.

"The memory of all that blood has haunted me and I never knew that my prayers were answered until I saw the commercial on NBC.

That's when I picked up my phone and made an appointment to donate blood."

It was so gratifying to know that I had made a difference like that. So many people don't donate blood just because it doesn't occur to them; it hasn't hit them in a personal way. Maybe they don't know anyone who's ever needed blood, maybe they figure enough other people do it so they don't have to. I wanted to be someone who could help wave the flag high to say that blood banks are almost *always* in need, and that people really do live or die based on whether or not there's enough blood available. Imagine if there had been a shortage before I arrived at the trauma bay.

"Maybe we can be blood sisters," she told me. "My blood type is a universal donor, so I can donate to anyone. Maybe you'll use my blood in one of your next surgeries."

The idea of "blood sisters" was beautiful to me. So many times lately, I wondered about the traits of the people who'd donated blood to me. When I accidentally left Jay-Z playing for an hour during a workout, I thought, *I don't like this music. Why didn't I change it?* and then my second thought was *I wonder if one of my blood donors likes this music.* Maybe there was just a *little* bit of hip-hop running through my veins now.

I did have two more surgeries that summer, which came with new scars, new rainbow-colored bruising, new pain, and new nausea. Each surgery, even the fairly minor ones, set me back again in my recovery, at least temporarily. The aftereffects of so much anesthesia were tough, and I just kept throwing my body new curveballs in what it would have to heal next—while it was already doing the hard work of healing the preexisting stuff: growing new skin, closing wounds, reawakening nerves and muscles. Every surgery was a source of anxiety, but I was also so glad to get them ticked off my to-do list—we were making improvements now.

One surgery was to retrieve my vena cava filter that had been placed there to help capture embolisms: blood clots that have broken away. I stayed awake with just mild pain management for this surgery.

The medical team put a blue cape around my neck and lifted it toward my head so I wouldn't see what was going on below me, like when a woman has a C-section—though the surgeon admitted that I was going to be the first patient of his to stay conscious during the procedure. It didn't scare me too much. I figured, when else would I ever have the opportunity to witness something like this? Plus, it made me feel pretty bad-ass to be able to say that I stayed awake during surgery. It would make for a great story.

Once they'd numbed the area as much as possible with an injection, the surgeon ran a long catheter through an incision in my neck. Then he inserted a long hooked wire into the catheter to retrieve the filter. I had asked for the remnants of previous surgeries—bones and things that they'd had to remove—but never got a yes before. This time they presented me with the inferior vena cava filter in a surgical cup. It looked like the metal structure of a teepee, with little chunks of tissue still clinging to it. (I still have it!)

When I finally removed the bandage from my neck, I realized I might have a better story to tell: There were two puncture holes that looked decidedly like a vampire bite worthy of a Hollywood movie.

While I was healing better than the doctors expected, that still didn't mean it was a smooth road. My skin was growing in, but it was paper thin and with no layer of fat underneath it, so it tore very easily. Just the elastic waistband of my underwear could open up the skin on my abdomen easily. And my leg was so stiff it was like a wooden leg...I had no range of motion because the skin was so taut and thin that if I moved freely, it just tore right open again. So despite gaining strength, I still needed to use canes and walkers because my gait was so thrown off and my leg motions were limited, making it easy for me to lose balance and hurt myself again.

The plan was to wait another few months and then start the process of expanding my "good" skin, then remove the paper-thin skin, stretching out the good parts to cover the gaps. I knew it was necessary, but I didn't want to do it anytime soon because it would mean going back to a wheelchair and starting new wound care all over again. I wanted to make some headway before that.

In September, I finally got my surgeon to agree that I could run and bike on an upright bike again.

"Can I sign up for a century ride?"

As my surgeon knew, a century ride meant one hundred miles within twelve hours.

"No century rides!"

"How far can I run?"

"I've learned to tell you to do a quarter of what you feel like you can do."

"So no marathons yet?"

"No. Start with a mile. See how it goes."

Hmph. Spoilsport.

It felt fitting, though, to take a ride with my sister-in-law Kaori.

It had been a year since our six-hundred-mile cycling tour together, and although I wasn't going to attempt that distance anytime soon, I did still want to celebrate with her that I could ride again. We rode on an abandoned rail trail that was away from any car traffic. At the halfway point, we stopped for lunch and were seated next to a sign that read:

TODAY IS A GIFT FROM GOD. REMEMBER TO THANK HIM.

I did.

Thank you, God, for my family, for my soul mate, for all of my doctors and medical team, for everything that's led to this moment. I am not okay yet, but I am getting there. I'm going to try to be that light that I know You want me to be. I will do it with Your help.

The more I intentionally focused on my gratitude, the less I focused on what I'd lost. As we closed in on the one-year anniversary of my trauma, we decided to throw a backyard thank-you party for all the medical people who had kept me alive and helped me to heal. I had forty invitations professionally printed and mailed, and eagerly awaited RSVPs. The first one came in.

"I'm just wondering... when the party is?" the nurse asked.

"What do you mean? Didn't you get the invitation?"

"Yes, but..." I'm sure she was being as delicate as possible. "It doesn't say."

I looked at the invitation again, and sure enough, no date or time was given. I imagined the recipients getting their invitations, shaking their heads, and saying, "Must be that girl who got run over by a freight truck, bless her heart."

It's true that my memory and judgment were still pretty off. I would make plans with a friend and completely forget by the next day. I would have no idea at all until she showed up, and I'd think it was a nice surprise, despite the fact that she'd told me exactly when she was coming one day earlier. It was a little unnerving to have it keep happening, and eventually Sean bought me a date book and helped me write everything down. I had also been telling reporters that I was thirty-eight years old; he finally helped me do the math to realize that I was thirty-seven. I'm not sure why I had skipped a year in my head.

The party was a great success. A local restaurant catered a soup bar, and we hired a bagpiper and drummer. Several of the medical staff were unable to be there because they had to be at work at the hospital, but my chief orthopedic surgeon delighted me by showing up on his bike, fully suited in cycling gear. I was so excited; it felt like a celebrity was rolling into my driveway. Unfortunately, his pager went off after a short time and he had to leave for the hospital.

We played boccie ball, volleyball, and croquet, and had a painting station for kids (and adults!). All around, it felt like a great way to say thank you to the people who'd kept me alive and helped me to get to my next birthday—a whole year of my life that wouldn't have happened without them. These were the people who'd made sure I still had a future to look forward to, and I'm glad I got to thank them.

After two appeals, I finally got approved for disability benefits, thanks to a lawyer friend who took on my case pro bono. The rule was that I could have a part-time job as long as I didn't earn more than $700 a month, so I applied for work at a shoe store for runners. They hired me and scheduled me for two to three shifts per week, during which I would help people get fitted for their shoes and ring up their purchases.

It quickly became apparent, though, that I was unable to work a cash register. I was no longer able to do basic math without severe panic attacks and help—I would take too long to figure it out, then give out the wrong change, and I could almost never reconcile my drawer at the end of my shift. Although she kept me around for several months anyway, the owner eventually stopped scheduling shifts for me, and Sean took me to a neuropsychologist for testing. It was then that I officially learned about my brain injury. After a barrage of scans and neurocognitive tests meant to check my long- and short-term memory, facial recognition, spatial references, and thinking skills, I received a report explaining where my weaknesses were—mostly things I had already realized, like the fact that I was mixing up words, but I hadn't thought deeply about the cause.

Interestingly enough, my brain injury wasn't from being run over; the doctors could tell from the area of the brain where the damage showed up that it was from the cardiac arrest afterward. Because I had been dead—twice—for a total of half an hour, my brain didn't get oxygen and brain cells started dying off. That's normal for cardiac arrest patients; lots of factors determine whether the prognosis will be good or bad, but it's unusual to ever have complete brain healing. Many brain injuries leave permanent effects, and most of the recovery is made in the first month or two.

Whether caused by football injuries, shaken baby syndrome, a car accident, drowning, or any number of other issues, brain injuries have the same wide-ranging symptoms: They can cause problems with thinking, memory, and reasoning; difficulty communicating appropriately; inappropriate social outbursts or aggression; personality changes; depression and anxiety; and problems with sensory processing—sight, sound, touch, hearing, and smell can all be "off." There are varying levels from mild to severe, and because of my helmet, mine was nowhere near as bad as it could have been if I'd had the double whammy of also dealing with trauma to the brain.

Just another thing I'm going to have to overcome, I thought. But this time, my athleticism wasn't going to be any extra help. Going to the gym couldn't bring back my math skills. I would have to just keep practicing and going to therapy, and hope my brain would continue doing its good work of putting itself back in order.

On September 20, I decided to tackle a major milestone: I wanted to drive by myself for the first time in almost a year. I had been cleared to drive for a few weeks, but I had to build myself up to the idea. Finally, one morning, I had a mission: I needed a new lightbulb, and I wanted to buy a mum to put by the front door. In total, I drove less than two miles, on non-busy roads, and I panicked, but I accomplished my mission. I even rewarded myself with a pumpkin spice latte from the Dunkin' Donuts up the block on my way home. *Shazam.*

Old me would never have understood why new me was celebrating something as simple as taking a quick drive, but when you're rebuilding your life from scratch, you have new standards for celebrating. This was a big deal. It meant I wouldn't be limited by my fear my whole life.

After another couple of quick trips, I decided that I would try to take a longer drive—appropriately enough, to therapy.

"I want to come to your office like a regular client," I told my therapist, who was still doing weekly home visits then.

"I'm all for it, but I have stairs leading up to my office. No elevator." She thought for a second. "Let me see if I can borrow an office on the ground floor for your visits."

That's what she ended up doing. She called later to tell me that she'd found an open office downstairs, and I could meet her there. So I set out to make this unfamiliar trip. I was nervous and hoping I wouldn't be too rusty—but I hadn't prepared myself for the sight I was about to see. As I turned left from my block onto Boston Post Road, there it was:

The stupid freight truck.

Not the same exact one, presumably, but the same company's truck. It was the first time I'd seen one of their trucks since the trauma. Panic overtook me and my breath caught in my throat. The truck pulled into an assisted-living facility's parking lot right in front of me, and something compelled me to follow it there. The driver was undoubtedly dropping off linens, but I was about to throw a bit of a wrench in his plans.

I didn't know exactly what my intention was at the time, but I had to see this truck up close. I parked my car next to it and walked right up to it, shaking and crying, as the driver headed around back to make his delivery. Then he spotted me and asked, "Ma'am, are you okay?"

I descended into sobs and screamed, "I was run over by one of these trucks!"

Then, by way of explanation, I lifted my shirt up over my abdomen.

He let out an involuntary curse.

"Do you see the tire marks?"

He nodded.

I rolled up the bottom of my pants to show him the bandaging on my leg.

"That's what the driver of one of these trucks did to me."

Quietly, he said, "What can I do for you?"

"Nothing. Just let me stand here."

"Take all the time you need."

He turned the engine off. I walked up to the front and opened up my arms to extend them over the entire double set of front tires. I wanted to feel them without being in danger, and to understand how wide they were together since I had their marks across my body. Then I reached down to let my fingers touch the places on my body where the tires ran me over, up to my sternum.

The driver asked, "When did this happen?"

"Almost a year ago."

"Do whatever you need to do."

I went to the back of the truck and ran my hands along the underside of those wheels and sobbed. I wanted to smell the tires, to feel the heat of the rubber friction and the underside of the truck again. I wanted to experience it all again in safety, as if I could defeat it this time. It felt like facing my demon in a very literal way. Instead of avoiding it, this time I was allowing myself to be vulnerable and running straight into and through the terror. This was the big beast that had almost taken my life.

This poor driver just stood there patiently, letting me cry. I don't know how long I was there, but finally, I asked, "Can I give you a hug?"

He didn't really answer and I did it anyway. I think I got the crazy-lady pass.

"Promise me that you will be really safe when you are driving this truck on the road, because one of your coworkers ran me over."

"I'm sorry. I absolutely will."

I got back into my car, still shaking, trying to pull myself together. I called Sean and he said, "Stay there. I'll pick you up."

"No, I'm going to continue driving to my appointment," I said.

Obviously, I was late. But my therapist understood and stayed late with me to work through what had just happened.

As difficult as it was to see that truck, it felt good afterward to have had that time to face it. There was nothing I could do to turn back time, but I would have to find ways to keep moving forward. Many days, I still felt like I was in a dark tunnel. The difference now was that I could not only envision a light at the end of it, but I could also see cracks all throughout the tunnel where light kept peeking through. People were my lights. The beautiful fall breeze on my face as I got back on my bike was a light. My ridiculous chickens were lights (even the one who turned out to be a rooster and began waking us at the crack of dawn).

And then another light came into our lives: We adopted an English Lab puppy and named her Jamis Malone. Jamis after the bicycle company.

Jamis was such a good little girl. She learned how to sit on command effortlessly, and spent all her sleep time snuggled up to big sister Sedona. I couldn't stop taking pictures of them together—it was just unbelievably cute. And considering I had been apprehensive about how Sedona might take to a new puppy, it was a relief to see she didn't mind too much.

We got a big crate, which looked funny with such a little puppy inside, and lined it with my old bed pads from Gaylord. All was well, except that Jamis was terrified of the rooster's crow and ran behind my legs, yelping. We knew we were going to have to find a new home for the rooster, and in the meantime, we put him in a crate in the shed each night to keep the crowing muted.

But our hearts were broken one October morning to find that an animal had gotten into the shed, knocked over his cage, and devoured him in the middle of the night. For all the noise he made, he was still a love, and I felt terrible that we hadn't been able to protect him.

October 8, 2012, was the one-year anniversary of my trauma, and also my day of rebirth—literally. I had come back to life twice that day, so it felt fitting to declare it a celebration-of-life day rather than think of it as a sad anniversary. Sean and I took a road trip to Vermont with the dogs that weekend. We went for a slow hike, then out to dinner. It was a crisp fall day with beautifully changing leaves, just as it had been a year prior, and I wasn't about to let bad memories steal my ability to make good new ones.

The next day, I found out that a local article had been published on the anniversary of my trauma stating that our police wanted to make Madison a more bike-friendly community, and that they were going to host a bike safety ride later in the month. I cried tears of joy when I read the article, knowing it was happening in part because of me.

Slowly but surely, I was also realizing that maybe Connecticut wasn't awful.

All these wonderful people who had saved my life lived in Connecticut. The neighbors who were now enthusiastically cleaning up the shoreline and helping us in any way they could, the facilities that had so capably cared for me, the adaptive sports program and bike safety clubs...they were all right here. Despite all my prejudices and anger about the place, I had come to the realization that this was home. I loved going back to visit Vermont, but I was no longer looking for an excuse to leave my new state.

Gaylord representatives had asked me to come speak at a staff luncheon they were having, so Sean and I drove there and I shared my story, the kind of care I got at Gaylord, and the good progress I'd made since then. It was empowering to get to tell my story in front of a room full of people at rapt attention, and afterward, several people came over to tell me that they were inspired by my words.

"You should become a motivational speaker," one said.

"You should write a book," another said.

Hmm! I always liked both speaking and writing, and had never shied away from giving talks for PeaceJam. Speaking about my own recovery was new, though. I thought about what was inspirational about it and ended up feeling even more appreciative of the care I'd received. If *anyone* had dropped the ball...I hated to think about the many, many ways I could have died.

I had constant reminders of how close I'd come. When I rolled over in bed, my sternum still made crackling noises. I'm sure that's from the CPR I received in the trauma unit. When CPR is done right, it can crack ribs or detach them from the sternum—it happens in about a third of all cases (more women than men), and a smaller percentage of people wind up with broken sternums. It's one of the things I always got questioned about when I taught CPR classes—people were very tentative about how hard to push.

"The person is already dead," I would tell them. "Yes, you may crack ribs. That's okay. They can live with cracked ribs. They can't live without breathing."

Now I was a living example of my own advice.

While I was at Gaylord, I got to visit my old room and its new inhabitant, a man just slightly older than I was. I saw the same desperate pain and fear in his eyes that once were in mine when I was in that same bed. I didn't get to learn his story, only to see that he was going through something awful. As I looked at him, I thought about what the audience members had said to me about using my story to inspire others. It made me want to reach out to him and everyone else in that place and tell them that there was hope beyond those walls. That as grim as the world looked right now, there was still beauty to be found. I wanted them to know that there were still sunrises and mountains and new puppies in the world, even if right now seemed to be a fog of never-ending pain.

My heart was heavy as I asked my friends to pray for him, that he be wrapped in angels' wings as he recovered from whatever it was that had happened to him. There were so many of us out there whose worlds had been ripped apart by one careless act, and I became more and more determined to serve as a positive force for all of us. I thought of how the woman in the running store had been so inspired by Matt Long's book that she bought it for a stranger—and how I, that stranger, had seen him as that same kind of beacon. I wondered if my own story would do that for someone someday.

I had no intention of being an Ironman like Matt, but I had every intention of pushing my limits to the max. That month, I ran my first relay marathon with the Red Cross team, which also included my physical therapist from Gaylord. In fact, she's the one who passed the baton to me. I was able to do a 5.8-mile leg of the race and then cross the finish line (this was just one year post-trauma), which was exhilarating! I earned a medal for our team's participation, and I made a decision then that I would never keep my medals: I would give them to my heroes instead. Shouldn't all heroes get medals?

I gave the first medal to my chief trauma surgeon, Dr. Kaplan. I loved seeing him smile as I put it around his neck and told him that he was my hero.

Finally, October 20 rolled around, and it was time for the cycling tour I'd organized. Sean and his fellow postal workers had delivered six thousand flyers around town, and there were posters up at Gaylord and local businesses. They let people know that the event was open to riders of all abilities and needs, and they could sign up for ten, twenty-five, or fifty miles along the Farmington Canal Heritage Trail.

The Madison police chief had registered to ride with me, and so had a few other officers. A friend's young son had offered to help "train" people by riding five miles with them as a school project. How awesome is that?

Prior to the tour day, Fox News invited me to appear live in their studio to talk about it. I'd never done a live show before and felt a little Mary Katherine Gallagher–ish about it all ("When I get nervous, I go like this..."). But it went well, and they agreed to come out to tape another segment on the morning of the ride.

Several longtime friends slept over at our house that weekend, which filled my heart with joy. It was amazing to have so many of us together under one roof for a cause I cared so deeply about. We had sixty participants on the day of the tour, and it was a big success: We raised just over $10,000 for the adaptive sports program. At an average cost of $2,000 per bike, that would mean five new bikes. There were three basic varieties: hand-pedaled bikes for people with spinal cord injuries; recumbent bikes for trauma survivors, amputees, and people who'd had strokes or balance impairments; and tandem bikes for people with visual impairments.

I wore my "Hope Rides Again," my favorite T-shirt post–brain surgery and now my favorite again. At the end of the day, I was exhausted and covered in bike chain grease, and so, so happy.

Having to say goodbye to all those friends at the end of it was the hardest part. But two weeks after it was over, I had already set the date for the next one: October 19, 2013, would be the second annual Gaylord Adaptive Sports Cycling Tour, and instead of raising money for more bikes, we'd branch out to fill the needs of their other programs: the Wounded Warrior Project, wheelchair rugby, adaptive downhill skiing, water skiing, archery, and more. The adaptive sports staff were such creative people, always finding new ways to make the impossible possible for people with physical limitations. They were a team I wanted on my side for a long time to come. Like me, they were determined to create light in the world.

Chapter 16

Racing On

THERE WERE SO MANY cycling and running events that one could sign up for, and I admit I may have gone a little crazy, but what better way to get my body moving and my endorphins kicking while also raising awareness and funding for good causes?

Another cause dear to my heart cropped up that November: Just before Thanksgiving, a Vermont friend's five-year-old daughter was diagnosed with a Wilms tumor, a form of kidney cancer. I decided to sign up for a half marathon that February in hopes of raising money toward her family's expenses as she began chemotherapy. I had two months to train, and I was finally able to start running without a walker. My first race without a walker was the Faxon Law New Haven Road Race, which I slowly ran wearing a sign pinned to my shirt that said THANK YOU, YALE MEDICAL STAFF, FOR SAVING MY LIFE!

When I finished, I ran straight over to the Yale Orthopedic Medicine tent and hugged the doctor. "I had my pelvis *screwed* back together! Just one year ago!" I said. "I still have a huge hole in my butt! I still have a giant eighteen-inch wound on my leg, and a hole in my abdomen, but I JUST RAN! HOW COOL IS RUNNING?"

And just like that, I loved running, after spending my whole life thinking of it as a chore. I still loved cycling, but it scared me. I didn't have the same bad memories attached to running. Now, when I ran, I felt the shadows of other people running alongside me...people I loved who couldn't be with me out on the trails. I thought about my grandparents, mostly. My grandfather, who worked tirelessly in his vegetable garden. My loving grandmother, who died on my birthday when I was in my early twenties. I didn't only think about people who had passed away, though. I also thought of my brother Erin, who had wanted to run with me but had ruptured his Achilles tendon and was stuck in bed. I thought about all the people who supported me and wanted to see me continue to heal and follow the path I had chosen. They were the shadows beside me the whole time, and they gave me strength to go on even when the pain verged on unmanageable.

My little puppy grew at an alarming rate, and I wondered if she was ready to become a training partner. She was soon able to hike with us, and also attempted to jog with me, but got overexcited about it and jumped up on me as if to say, *"Mom, this is so awesome!"* I wondered if there was such a thing as athlete/dog training classes to get us in better lockstep. In the meantime, I figured I'd better stick to Sean and my girlfriends.

I wasn't ready to ride a bike on roads, except during group rides where I felt safer in a pack. Even then, there was a point in every ride when panic overwhelmed me and I broke down. The memories were still too fresh; every car on the road was now my potential enemy. Just the sound of engines nearby made my heart race and my throat tighten. For the most part, I stuck to riding stationary bikes indoors and trail riding. It was a loss, but I had to honor what felt safe to me.

I was even jumpy when I was out running. One night, while I was training for the half marathon, I ran through a park. In the last mile, a car came toward me, headlights beaming. I ran into the grass in terror, and the car stopped. The driver yelled something at me, and I went straight into fight-or-flight mode. I chose flight! I ran full speed with the power of panic fueling me, worrying that I was about to get thrown into the back of some crazed murderer's truck. The driver pulled up behind me and I was terrified that he was following me.

It turned out to be a park ranger.

"Park's closed, ma'am."

I couldn't even breathe.

"Is that... what you yelled back there?"

"Yes, it is. Didn't think you heard me. You were all lit up like a Christmas tree. Sorry if I scared ya. I just got to do my job and keep people out of the park at night."

I was awfully glad that no one had videotaped my reaction to the park ranger, because I'm pretty sure it would have given people a good laugh to see me scream like a B-movie horror film actress over absolutely nothing.

Panic attacks do that to you. They make you hypervigilant, ready to pounce at the slightest provocation. Your brain is conditioned to believe that there are threats all around you and that you need to be ready to fight them or flee quickly. Even things you logically know are safe can cause physical reactions that you can't control—racing heart, tight chest, sweaty palms, feelings of depersonalization (like everything is a movie), nausea, dizziness, shaking, numbness, or tingling...in short, anything that reminded me of my trauma in even the smallest way could set my body off to react just the same as if I were freshly experiencing an actual trauma. Lots of people wind up in the emergency room thinking they're having a heart attack, only to be told it's "just" a panic attack. It's hard to believe because the symptoms are real, no matter how they're triggered.

It was unfair to have to deal with this kind of psychological torment, but then again, a lot of things were unfair in life. I thought a lot about how unfair it was for a five-year-old to have to deal with cancer, and I hoped I could raise enough money to make a difference for her family. Maybe it would give her parents the ability to take time off from work the way Sean had in the early days when I was at my worst. I thought of the ways friends had pulled together to help me, and now that I was improving, I wanted to find a way to pay that forward and help others.

Just as I was planning this, though, tragedy ripped through our community in an almost unspeakable way.

On December 14, 2012, a twenty-year-old man killed his mother and then opened fire at Sandy Hook Elementary School, killing twenty children and six staff members. All of the children were six or seven years old. Nothing could explain it; it was one of the cruelest, most senseless acts I'd ever heard of, and it was far too close to home.

My community reeled from the news. At a Red Cross blood drive a week later, I encountered a man in his midtwenties with heavy eyes. Most of us in Connecticut were pretty lost that week, but he just looked broken in a way beyond the rest of us. I introduced myself, thanked him for donating blood, and asked him how he was doing.

"I just buried my dad two weeks ago because of brain cancer, and now I just buried my best friend who was shot at Sandy Hook while protecting her students. I think I'm numb, and all I know how to do right now is be here."

He pulled out his phone and showed me photos of his father smiling just weeks before his death, and a photo of himself with his dear friend Victoria Soto just a week and a half prior, smiling together. All I could do was wrap my arms around him. I thought it was beautiful that in this time of distress, his way of coping was to donate blood to help others.

He knew who I was, and told me, "Your story inspires me; it gives us all hope."

All I could respond with was what I was actually grappling with: "Sometimes it doesn't feel fair that I lived and so many die."

I wanted to believe that saving me was part of God's plan, but I also couldn't accept that God didn't have a good plan for those twenty-six children and women. It was something so cruelly unfathomable, and brought me right back to the reason I had started working with PeaceJam, to combat violence and bring about more humanity and understanding.

Although I was no longer working for the organization in any official capacity, I still greatly supported the work PeaceJam did. It had been such a huge part of my life, and its mission still resonated with me. I wanted to continue doing good work like I had with PeaceJam, but for now, the best way I could figure was to keep my name in the news so that I could keep promoting causes I cared about.

Because it was difficult to train in the winter, when the roads and bike paths turned to ice or slush, my surgeon finally gave me (tepid) permission to start swimming in pools again, so Sean and I headed to the YMCA after dinner one night. As I was getting my towel in the locker room, a little girl about six years old came around the corner and looked at me.

"Were you hurt?" she asked.

"Yes," I told her. "I was hit by a car."

She peppered me with questions as her younger sister, about four years old, walked right over to me and ran her little fingers down the scars on my legs. With sweet innocence, the two of them continued asking me questions—"Did you cry when that happened? Does it still hurt? What does that feel like?"—and touching my scars. Their mother heard me explaining and walked over, apologizing for her daughters' forwardness.

Then she paused a second. "Are you Colleen?" she asked.

When I responded, "Yes," she began crying through her smile.

"Girls, this is Colleen...the cyclist who almost died who we prayed for every night before bed."

The girls smiled and the older one said, "So God listened."

The mother had seen my story in the newspaper and the family had been praying for me for months. The girls' sweet little hands and wonderfully innocent eyes were so healing. They both hugged me and I thanked them.

"You're a miracle," the little girl said. "Mommy said you died two times and needed a whole lot of blood. Where did they put the blood into you?"

I showed them all of my port scars.

"Colleen, do you still cry from all the pain?" the little one asked.

"Yes," I said.

"Colleen, why do people hurt each other?"

That's when my tears fell. I wondered how much they knew about Sandy Hook, or of all of life's injustices and tragedies.

"Because some people are very sad and hopeless and they don't know how to love, and that is why it is so important that girls like you exist in this world, to share love and prayers and be a light."

We hugged again and they left. I took my towel down and walked with my head held high to the pool area, feeling so healed by these little souls who had prayed for me before they'd ever met me.

In January, we took a whirlwind trip to Florida to celebrate Sean's fortieth birthday. My rock, my best friend, had done so little for himself in the last year. He'd been on a surfboard once all year. So we took a mini-vacation to the Florida Keys, where we went cycling across almost 120 miles of bike trails. He had freshly short hair after growing it out all year to donate to Locks of Love, and I couldn't get over how handsome he looked.

When we got back home, we ran into a teacher we knew at the local Stop & Shop. Her school did an outstanding job with student blood drives, and Sean and I had come to thank the students for leading the state of Connecticut.

"It's so good to see you guys!" she said as we greeted each other in the produce aisle.

We started with small talk about the school, and she thanked us for showing up to talk to the kids. "We love you guys. The kids admire you so much for the way you're fun and honest with them. It's amazing that both of you needed blood donations."

Somehow that led to a question about Sean's accident. He promptly lifted up his shirt to show her his scars.

"I was impaled from back to front, and I needed a colostomy, too," he added. "So we have matching colostomy scars!"

He started to lift my shirt to show her.

Under my breath, I muttered, "Please don't lift my shirt up."

"Well, her scar goes up and down while mine goes across, so if you squish our bellies together, it makes a plus sign!" he helpfully explained.

We were so accustomed to talking openly by then that he just let it all hang out—the open abdominal wounds, the way colostomies work—and she suddenly turned pale. Though Sean is color-blind, even he could see that her lips were turning blue.

"I think I'm passing out," she said, and sure enough, she did. Sean hurried behind her and hooked underneath her arms to guide her to the floor as her legs gave out from under her. I took her vitals and helped to prop her up. She was out for only a few seconds, and when she came to again, she was very embarrassed.

"I just get so queasy. I know this happens to me. I shouldn't have had this conversation," she said.

We drove her home because it was clear she wasn't going to do any more grocery shopping that day, and we learned two things: One, Sean and I make a damn good emergency team, and two, not everyone can handle details, even if they ask.

I was reminded of that again a few weeks later when I was invited to speak at Salisbury School, an all-boys private high school. There were 375 boys in the audience; they were future surgeons, engineers, CEOs, musicians, and pilots, and they were listening. I described in detail what had happened to me, and when I began listing my injuries—the pelvic break, the skin ripped off my abdomen and leg and "feminine region," the crooked ankle—I saw a boy with his head in his hands looking like he was very woozy.

"You okay?" I called out. "Deep breaths."

From the nervous mumbling around the room, I realized several of them needed a break. So we all took some deep breaths and put our arms up in the air before I went on.

"I'm not going to tell you any more gross stuff," I promised.

But I did tell them about what happened when I ran out of blood and died on the table: "It's kind of like when you're changing a fish tank and you take all the water out, but you forget to unplug the filter. So the filter just runs and starts getting louder and louder because it's trying to suck the water but it can't. Before you know it, the motor burns out. That's what happened to my heart."

Then I told them about my depression, because it's important for people young and old to talk about that. It's great to hear about success stories and people who've had amazing outlooks on difficult circumstances, but not everyone comes through trauma feeling ready to skip down the road and sing. I told them how down I was, and that I needed to "get out of my head." And then I told them about how I found gratitude again by focusing on my heroes.

How fortuitous was it that the head surgeons from every major department just happened to all be working that Saturday? And that there was enough type O blood available for me, considering there was no time to test to find out what my blood type was? I explained in detail how important blood donations were and how any one of them could be a hero, too.

Those boys were engaged. They were attentive and full of emotion, and when it was all over, I knew that they were now not only future surgeons and CEOs...they were also future blood donors.

Sean and I continued to run together to train for the half marathon, and in the hopes of working our way back up to doing full marathons and triathlons together again. I had good and bad days; one day I was in so much pain that I had to stop and walk the rest of the way, and I was momentarily very upset about it. Then I put it in perspective for myself; no one had been sure I was ever even going to walk again. Every step I took was a miracle. The fact that I was training for a half marathon was almost unbelievable.

My brother Erin had coined the phrase "Kelly Strong" to describe our family—he had overcome sarcoidosis (the same disease that killed Bernie Mac), a torn Achilles tendon, and a myriad of other issues while working full-time, raising three awesome boys, and being a husband and best friend to his wife. I leaned on his descriptor some days. I was strong. Slow and strong. In pain and strong. Sometimes terrified and strong. Whatever else I was, I was also Kelly Strong.

I took that strength with me to New York City that February, where we loaded up on the best carbs around (pizza and bagels) before we ran the Central Park Half Marathon to fundraise for Rowan. Throughout the hilly course, a guide from Achilles International named Adam Meyer accompanied and encouraged me. We ended up with more than $2,000 to donate to the family, and a new finisher medal to present to Rowan, for fighting her battle with cancer.

The next race was a very big deal to me, too: The Central Park Half Marathon, where I ran with Sean and Gail as my guides, and for the last three miles, Matt Long (author of the book that inspired me) joined me. What a thrill! I decided I was through being apologetic about my slow times, and that I could deal with whatever pain came afterward. After all, like C. Hunter Boyd said, "Last is just the slowest winner." I felt more alive than I had since the trauma; I felt like me again. This medal went to my SICU nurses at Yale.

I kept signing us up for more races, and I was so glad that I had a husband who understood this sort of thing. Most of them went without a hitch (pain, yes, but whatever), but every now and then my body just wouldn't cooperate.

I was sick all of March with a lupus flare-up and a chest infection, but I was able to get on with it anyway. Things came to more of a head in April. My blood pressure was spiking, but because of my ongoing panic attacks and pain, it was hard to distinguish that from other causes. If I went running to a doctor every time I had a symptom, I would have been at the doctors' offices every single day. It took a lot to make me seek help, but that day finally came when, the morning before a half marathon, I couldn't get out of bed. I was exhausted and had a fever, terrible back pain, and nausea. Then came the nonstop vomiting. I vomited often because of all the scar tissue built up in my stomach, but this was a bit much even for me. Sean took me to the emergency room, where—after a four-hour wait—we found out I had an enlarged, blocked, infected kidney that would need to be seen by a surgeon the next week.

"But if I'm feeling better, can I still run my half marathon tomorrow?" I asked the doctor.

She stared at me blankly. "You need to take it easy," she said.

"How about if I just do the five-K portion of it?"

I have no idea why she said yes, except that she consulted with my trauma surgical team and they probably told her that I was going to do it anyway. I was feeling a bit better by the next morning, so I went ahead and ran the 5K and then made it to the finish line with my camera so I could video Sean's half-marathon finish: an impressive 1:52 on a very hilly course in Danbury, Connecticut.

Despite my physical setbacks, two wonderful things happened for us that month: We were having so much fun with our puppy, Jamis, that we decided to adopt another golden Lab, Coda, named after the kind of Jamis bicycle I'd been riding; and my leg wound closed up enough that my wound care was able to be completed with just two giant Band-Aids and Neosporin. Just like that, $400 worth of wound care supplies each month were no longer needed. It felt like freedom. After almost two years, I could exhale and stop doing wound care until another surgery.

We took the dogs to the beach to celebrate. Amazingly, adding another pet to our household was so easy: All three dogs and the cat got along just fine. Sedona's health was up and down—some days she wouldn't eat; other days she scarfed down donuts and ham with enthusiasm. Basically, I would tempt her with anything just as long as she would eat. I knew we were nearing the end of the road, but I kept looking into those eyes of hers and trusting that she would tell me when it was time. I didn't want to keep her in prolonged pain, but I also didn't want to give up on her too soon. I knew what it was like to beat the odds, and I figured my dog did, too.

My next surgical team appointment didn't bring the greatest news. They determined that I was going to have some level of incontinence for the rest of my life. And when I say "incontinence," I'm not talking about peeing.

So...yeah.

It really wasn't sexy, and the idea that I was not going to be able to control my own poop *forever* was damn depressing. But that's not where the bad news ended.

"Colleen, your kidney is dying," my urologist told me. "I think the scar tissue is closing off its ability to do its job and if we don't do something soon, we will need to just remove it."

"What options do I have?"

"I want you in surgery on Friday. We can try inserting a stent into the kidney, through the ureter, and into the bladder to see if that improves functionality."

It wasn't much of a choice; of course I needed to try whatever he suggested to keep my kidney. We had also seen the fertility team at Yale, who clearly determined we needed to use a surrogate if we still wanted a baby. It was a lot of finality at once, and hard to take in.

Carrying a baby was just one way of becoming a mom, I knew, and there were other options in the world...but they weren't my chosen options. I had always dreamed of what it would be like to have a big, round belly, feel little baby kicks. Despite knowing on some level that my body was torn apart in all the wrong places, I had still held out some hope for a miracle. This marked the end of hope. It was one more thing I'd never have, and one more thing I couldn't do for Sean.

Even though I had successfully changed my overall focus from depression to gratitude, that didn't mean every day was perfect. I still had lots of days when a lesser emotion bubbled to the top. Anger, sadness, loss, jealousy. Each time, I'd have to fight my way through the feelings and choose a different one as soon as I was able to refocus. It would have been easy to stay stuck on all I'd lost, but what good would that have done me?

The more good I did in the world, the less time I had to feel bad for myself, so I just kept finding ways to be useful. I visited a food bank and noticed how much processed, canned food they had on their shelves.

"Do you ever get any fresh produce?" I asked the man running the place.

"Nah. Too expensive," he said.

"How about if I grow some fresh vegetables from my garden and I bring them to you in the mornings on the day the pantry is open?"

"You're going to grow food for other people?"

"Yeah!" I said.

I knew that if I started now, within two months some people who would ordinarily get a selection of mostly unhealthy goods would get a beautiful bounty like what we ate—the foods that helped to heal me. The right food is so good for not only the body, but the mind, too. People who are dealing with hard times should get good nutrients, I figured.

It gave me an outward place to focus when my inward focus got too scary. As I headed into my nineteenth surgery in nineteen months, I thought, *I should be used to this by now.* But I'm not sure if you ever get used to the idea of being unconscious and losing control of your body. Once again, I would be under anesthesia, counting on the surgeons to have steady hands and know just what to do, and for my body to react as well as possible without complications.

When I woke up, the news wasn't great. They had succeeded in inserting a stent to open the pathway from my kidney to my bladder, but they'd also found massive scar tissue from the trauma, and that would require a longer, more extensive surgery soon. This would be a stopgap measure, and there was uncertainty about how effective it would be. We'd know in a couple of weeks, after follow-up testing. In the meantime, I now had a ten-inch tube inside me that was a whole new source of pain.

I hoped the pain was just temporary and would ease up as soon as my body got used to it, but nope. Every time I laughed, jogged, sneezed, or did anything else that moved my belly, it felt like I was getting stabbed. Intimacy with my husband, which had been off the table ever since the trauma, was pushed back even further. I felt so frustrated that there was something else standing in the way of being with the man who had done so much for me.

The things that were happening medically were in such stark contrast to the other things in my life at the time. I got a phone call out of the blue one day from a producer of *The Dr. Oz Show*, asking if I would come on the show to talk about my experiences. I assume they learned about me from local media. I was not a daytime television watcher, so I didn't know much about the show except what I'd heard from relatives, but I recognized a good opportunity when I heard one.

They sent a crew out to my house first to film the intro and commercials, and it was a great experience. It ran much longer than they had originally told me: eight hours of filming, which I knew would have to be whittled down to just a brief segment. Then we headed to New York City, where the show put us up in a terrific hotel for the night before the taping.

I met Dr. Oz in the hallway the morning of the show, and he told me that I was an inspiration.

"Do you know my story?" I asked.

"Yes, I know you died," he said.

"Do you know how I died?"

"I know you got run over by a truck."

"Okay, sorry. Just checking," I said with a smile. I knew television personalities are busy people, and I didn't know how much prepping they got.

After that, I was sent to hair and makeup, where I was curled and sprayed as a man came and sat down next to me and said, "Hi! I'm the expert."

That confused me. "Expert what?"

"I'm an expert on the afterlife."

"Oh. Did you die?"

"No, but I've researched it extensively and written books about it. I've had several patients who've died and come back, too."

"So your work is based on . . . ?"

"I think there's some good, strong data."

I had no idea there was going to be an "afterlife expert" on the segment, and I have to admit I was skeptical about the idea. I just hoped it would be an accurate depiction of what I'd gone through.

The on-set interview lasted about half an hour, and I told Dr. Oz about all I'd gone through on that day—the terrible fear, the pain, the awareness of what was happening around me and how hard I fought not to die. We talked about my heroes, and how I now worked with the Red Cross to encourage blood donations, and about my commitment to advocating for bike safety and safer roads. I left feeling pretty good about it all, but also nervous about how it would be edited.

My episode, "What Comes After Death?" aired on May 15, 2013. All that we had recorded was whittled down to just a few questions that highlighted one small piece of my experience: the time in the ambulance when I felt warm and safe. Without a doubt, that was a meaningful spiritual moment for me, but it was thirty seconds. The rest of the time, I was terrified, in severe pain, and aware that I was dying. The show seemed to want to paint a more comforting picture of how we die.

I was still thankful to have had the chance to talk about my story on a national level, but I was frustrated that the things I cared about were left on the cutting room floor.

"They didn't talk about blood donations or bike safety at all," I said to Sean.

"We'll know better next time," he said.

I decided that from then on, I wouldn't agree to do interviews like that unless they were live, or unless I had some measure of control over the final edits. It was still a good experience in many ways, though, especially because I had so many people from all over the country contact me afterward to ask questions or say they were inspired by my story. My Facebook page was slammed with requests, which made me a little self-conscious; I've always been a very open sharer, so I wasn't so sure I should let hundreds of strangers into my life that closely. I started a public "fan page" for that purpose instead.

Soon I was also featured in *Runner's World*, which was a thrill, and *Connecticut Magazine* named me as one of the year's top "40 Under 40" movers and shakers. Both magazines sent photographers, and I wore a belly-baring running outfit for the *Runner's World* shoot. My scars and body imperfections were going to be on full display, which made me nervous, but I also knew that the magazine would do a respectful job. I had earned my right to be seen as an athlete despite all those scars.

The scars on the outside weren't the worst of my problems. A couple weeks after my surgery, my urologist called at 9:15 p.m., which is never a good sign, to let us know that the procedure hadn't worked. The follow-up testing revealed that my right kidney was functioning at less than 10 percent of normal capacity, which meant that I now had ten inches of tubing in my body and had gone through another surgery for nothing. They were considering removing the kidney altogether in the next surgery. Most people can live with one kidney, but of course it's a risk. Even worse was the news that if my left kidney failed, I wouldn't be eligible for a donor kidney because of my extensive pelvic damage.

"What next?" I asked him.

"We'll reassess in two months with another scan. If you're still at ten percent or below, then we need to remove it."

"Is this going to limit me in any way in the meantime? Can I still be as active as I am?"

"Live the life you were meant to live."

I loved that he said that.

Once again, the news was a lot to take in, and I was glad I had things to get my mind off it. I cooked up a storm—garlic lentils, asparagus and goat cheese soup, wheat berries with herbs, roasted vegetables, a green salad, and fresh bread—and invited company over. I didn't want to dwell on bad news. I wanted to live the life I was meant to live.

With that in mind, I signed up for my first post-trauma triathlon, the "Oh My Goddard!" Olympic Triathlon in Rhode Island. One of the biggest dangers to me was the contact that often happens during an open swim. As people jockey for position, arms and legs go flailing everywhere, and it's very normal to get kicked or hit in the face or body. I was very nervous about getting nailed in my good kidney, so Sean agreed to be my "bodyguard." He would swim next to me and make sure no one got too close.

He ended up taking quite a few hits himself—what he called "taking one for the team"—leaving me unscathed. The triathlon committee was nervous about my being a liability, but there were already so many barriers to people of different abilities being able to compete—I didn't want to have to argue with the committee over what I might need. I knew I'd be okay with Sean by my side. I called him my "eagle" for all the ways he guided me, and for his big "wingspan."

In the end, despite a lot of the usual pain, cramping from the kidney and bladder stent, a couple of wound changes, and needing some extra assistance getting onto the bike, I finished that race.

"You are an Olympic triathlete!" Sean told me. "I'm so proud of you."

You know what? I was pretty proud of me, too. And I still looked good in a wetsuit.

Chapter 17

Rainbow Bridge

I DIDN'T THINK I WOULD ever have a harder day than October 8, 2011, but then came June 26, 2013, the day I finally had to say good-bye to Sedona. She had been my steadfast companion for thirteen years, and as I watched her lie on the floor, panting and drooling, I felt selfish for wanting to keep her longer. She could no longer see or hear, she rarely wanted to eat, and it was difficult for her to walk. She just didn't seem to enjoy anything anymore. The puppies did a good job of tending to her when they thought she needed care, but it wasn't any kind of life for Sedona.

My heart was shattered as I brought her to our trusted vet, knowing that I was doing the right thing, but nevertheless feeling miserable about it. She had been my best friend through so many changes and life phases, so many new places. She'd made friends at my work, alerted me when I was about to have a seizure, gone running and hiking and swimming at the beach with me, and snuggled me through every broken heart. How do you say goodbye to a dog that special?

I was thankful to her vet for being so respectful, and I watched Sedona take her last breath with a sunbeam touching her forehead. I prayed that she was in a better place where she could see and hear again, where she would run along the beach and eat ice cream to her heart's content.

The next morning, once the rain cleared, I went for a run... and I had a new shadow by my side. Then I kissed my puppies and made them promise to stay young forever.

It was tough to do much of anything that week, but I kept my body moving anyway. The cadence of the bike was always soothing, despite everything. Just the rhythm of it was meditative for me. The rest of the world would fall away with every circle, circle, circle.

I decided to take on a new challenge: my first solo road race in two years. Sean had to work the day of the race. Normally I just wouldn't have signed up, but this time I knew I was ready to test the waters. I signed up as an able-bodied athlete and didn't let on what had happened to me. Shortly before the race, I had my stent removed, so at least there was one source of pain that wouldn't be there this time.

After I signed in and prepared to run, two different volunteers approached me to ask if I was sure I should run in my condition... they were referring to the fact that I was limping. If they only knew!

As I ran the course, a race official called out to me, "No wonder you're so slow—you're smiling! Fast runners don't smile. You can pick it up!"

"Actually, I can run, so I smile," I said.

I came in sixth to last. The following day, I topped myself: I did the Rhode Island Crabman, my first solo triathlon in years. Sean was there, but competing at his own pace this time. We were so thrilled to have finished and didn't hear the news until the following day that a seventy-year-old athlete had died of a heart attack during the swim portion of the race. It was awful to find out, and the only thing that brought me any comfort was the idea that he went out doing something he loved.

It was something *I* loved, too, which was partly why I was ignoring phone calls from Yale...they were calling to try to schedule my kidney surgery, and I knew that meant six weeks of no exercise afterward, not to mention whatever side effects might come along. I was in such a good groove that I didn't want to have to interrupt it. I also didn't know if I was ready to face the idea of losing my kidney. It had become symbolic in my mind—we had lost the ability to have a baby because of the trauma, and now I had this other piece of me to protect. In a strange way, it became like protecting an unborn baby. I didn't want it to die inside me, and I didn't want to wake up to the news that I'd lost something else forever.

Finally I emailed my chief surgeon to ask if I could postpone it a bit, since I'd just been under anesthesia three months ago. "Sorry if I'm being whiney," I added.

He simply wrote back, "Have some cheese with that whine and get the surgery scheduled."

That's it. No frills. That's why he was a trauma surgeon and why I was lucky to have him as my quarterback. I got the stupid surgery scheduled. It was also why it was so hard to hear that, the following week, Dr. Kaplan was leaving Connecticut to go to Pennsylvania to work at a veterans' trauma hospital. Without his decision not to give up on me even after twenty minutes of CPR and then a second round of ten minutes of CPR, I would not be here. I knew that Yale would bring in another experienced trauma surgeon, but I was sure going to miss him.

To prove it, I had a parting gift for him. Sean and I did the craziest thing we'd done thus far: We signed up for the Timberman half Ironman event in New Hampshire: a 1.2-mile swim, 56-mile bike ride, and 13.1-mile run. It was unprecedented. Even before my trauma, I'd never done a half Ironman, so why did I think I could do one now? I just knew that I was on a roll, breaking down all kinds of personal barriers, and I had to give it a try. I was completely ecstatic and terrified to push myself to such an extreme. My goal was simply to finish the race and give my medal to Dr. Kaplan.

Two weeks before the race, Sean and I journeyed up to New Hampshire to scope out the setting and practice some of the route. While we were there, I scattered some of Sedona's ashes at the start and finish of the swim and at the finish chute area so she could be part of the day with me. She had been my swimming buddy prior to the trauma, and I was still grieving her immensely.

At every Ironman event, there is a company that makes display pieces for the medals. They show off the medal and the route, and include a plaque with custom engraving of your name, your finish time, and anything else you want to write. It was a leap of faith to hand out our credit card information before the race to reserve one of these display pieces, and I was a little nervous that I was jinxing myself by doing it—but I did it anyway.

We woke up at 3:45 on the morning of the race, and I knelt and prayed. I thanked God that I was there, that this was happening, and that I had this honor. I prayed I would stay safe and hoped that my choice was wise.

I met with my guide, Chris, one of countless volunteers from Achilles International who trains and races beside people with disabilities to keep us safe and help us maintain our quality of life as athletes. Not all disabled athletes need guides, but because I was still fragile and unsteady on my feet, I did. I had to denote that I needed a guide when I signed up, and he had to register, too. He wore a bright yellow Achilles Guide top, and he would do the entire race alongside me to keep me protected.

There are good people all around, I remembered. I added Chris to my list of heroes. What a wonderful thing to do for someone—to use a skill of yours to lift up another person and help them achieve something they couldn't safely do alone.

Just as I was getting psyched up in the starting area for the swim, the announcer's voice came across the intercom:

"We have a special first-timer amongst us today named Colleen Kelly Alexander. Just two years ago, she was run over by a multi-ton freight truck and ripped apart. She required over seventy-eight blood transfusions, was in a coma over a month, and is here today to give thanks for her life and show the strength that blood donors give when they roll up their sleeves."

I started shaking. Ironman seeks motivational moments to share with athletes before the gun goes off, but no one had asked me if they could make that announcement. I was trying to blend in with the masses as much as possible with my guide, Chris, and now all eyes were on me as I walked up to the disabled athlete swim start. My heart raced and tears of anxiety welled up. Luckily, there wasn't much time to feel self-conscious before the starting gun went off.

As we swam over the lake bed and looked down on the sand glistening in the sunlight, I imagined Sedona swimming beside me with her big goofy face, barking and splashing in the water, maneuvering around with her giant, otter-like Lab tail. I knew that some of the glistening I was seeing came from her bone fragments, and as much as that made it hard, I found comfort in my soul having her present and swimming with her again.

Chris maintained my pace the entire swim and guarded me beautifully from being hit, punched, or kicked. At the end of the swim, I was disoriented and struggled getting my "land legs," so Chris picked me up under my arms and helped me into the transition area, where my next helper, John Young, was standing by my bike with an immense smile.

John has dwarfism. He's four foot four. I'd had no idea who would be there to help me with balance and to get my wetsuit off, stand guard as I did wound changes, and help me into my bike clothes. John's arms were outstretched and he cheered me on with this resoundingly powerful voice, "Colleen! Let's go! I'm John and I'm here to help! You tell me what to do!"

I had never been face-to-face with a little person before. He was larger in life than anyone I had met.

"Please hold my waist firmly so I don't fall over," I said, and I began pulling my wetsuit down.

"Well, this is an awkward way to meet!" he said, and we both burst out laughing. Once I got my wetsuit down around my feet, he held on to my waist tighter and I wrapped my arms around his shoulders and pulled my legs up so the wetsuit snapped off from around my ankles.

Then he helped me into my dry bike shorts and handed me my clean wound bandaging as he continued smiling and encouraging me. My transition time was close to ten minutes that day, which is an exceedingly long amount. However, when he unracked my bike and handed it to me and said, "Go get 'em!" I felt so peaceful and thankful. We didn't know it then, but in 2016, John would be the first athlete with dwarfism to complete a full Ironman, at the age of fifty.

At the bike mount, Chris held on to both of our bikes and stabilized me while helping to lift my leg up and over the handlebars so I didn't fall over. I still couldn't mount or dismount the bike solo because of my lack of range of motion and balance issues.

The fifty-six-mile bike ride was challenging, but powerfully epic: beautiful views, beautiful climbs, and wildly scary descents. Chris rode directly behind me in case my legs weakened and I lost the ability to go into full rotations. If that were to occur, he could grab the back of my seat and help me up the hills as he rode beside me so I wouldn't crash and fall over (something I had done only once before this day post-trauma, and needed to make sure I didn't do again—orthopedic surgeons aren't fans of having their handiwork messed with).

When we crossed the bike dismount line I was in tears. All I had left was a half marathon. I needed to change my wound dressings, which had soaked with body fluids again, change my bike shorts, which were soaked with some blood and bodily fluids, and put on clean compression shorts. I couldn't run well unless I had tight enough compression shorts on, as my glutes had been literally ripped out from the inside and pulled apart. Although the hole was closing up, the muscles and everything inside still felt like giant bags of heavy, wet sand sloshing around on my bones. The only way I could engage my butt muscles well enough to run was to have those babies strapped tight up onto my skeletal frame.

Right away on the run, I was hurting. My legs didn't seem to want to engage, my body overheated, I felt nauseated, and the thought of trying to run 13.1 miles after all that swimming and biking was terrifying.

One step at a time, I reminded myself.

I remembered the young man at Gaylord with the severe spinal cord injury who would probably never walk again. I thought about all the people who were important to me, all the people who gave me CPR and donated blood, my husband's huge smile through tears as he said, "You and me, love, you got this." I knew that when I crossed, he would have finished hours earlier and would be standing there so full of pride (and probably a bit relieved to see me upright).

The run became a walk/jog. I had to stop every ten to fifteen steps to have Chris stretch my legs and put pressure on my back and different areas of my body to relieve the pain. When we came into the finish chute, most of the race had begun closing down, but we crossed that finish line with a time of eight hours, forty-eight minutes.

I hugged Chris, standing up as strong as I could, and cried. Sean stood there screaming, "YES! YES!" We took photos and I thanked God. Within a few minutes, though, I began crashing hard. Something was wrong.

I looked at Sean and said, "I feel like I'm in a dream. Everything is distant-feeling and I'm shaky."

He walked me to the med tent, where my legs and arms started convulsing intensely. I was so scared. Sean explained my trauma history. They removed my bandages and rebandaged me, warmed my body, and encouraged me to try to drink as much fluid as possible. A woman walked in and asked if she could lay hands on me and perform qigong, a type of energy work. She massaged my body and prayed, saying, "I feel God's presence with us. I know you are meant to do great things." I knew God sent her to be with me at that very moment.

I stayed in the med tent for more than an hour getting fluids and body work while speaking to this angel, who I would later learn was the head of post-race care for Timberman. She also taught energy work and massage. I knew I had to go back and race again, and she would get my next medal.

Going to bed that night was such a satisfying feeling; it was my biggest athletic accomplishment, and I'd done it less than two years after the trauma. I was starting to believe that I was meant for great things after all.

I believed it even more when I saw my sixty-one-year-old neighbor running down the road two days later. I pulled my truck over.

"You're running!" I screamed.

"I haven't run in thirty years, but I figured if you can do an Ironman, then I can start running."

I threw my arms around her in gratitude. She had started running right after hearing about my finish. It was the best topper to that day I could have gotten.

Over the next year, I would get to celebrate many times as several family members also took up running and joined me for races—notably, my nephew Zachary was my partner for the Disney half marathon, the slowest half marathon I've ever run but also the most fun. We kept stopping for hugs and pictures, and he said, "Aunt Colleen, thanks for getting me into running. Thank you for letting me do this race with you. You and I are awesome."

We completely were. The medal I earned from that half marathon went to his little brother, Anthony. My nephews were always some of my biggest cheerleaders and made me feel so special. I knew they had been praying daily for me, and I wanted Anthony to know what a hero he was to me for believing in the power of prayer. Little did I know that Zachary would become a serious athlete, running a 5:30 mile on the high school track team just three years later.

I scheduled three more triathlons before the September surgery date, along with another half marathon, a 20K, and a 10K, figuring I wanted to get my body into the best shape possible for this next round of anesthesia. My next medal went to two more of my heroes: my parents. Then I promised my next medal to Pem McNerney, the reporter who had first covered my story as I lay comatose at Yale, and who had long since become a true friend. She had taken such care to learn about my background and my aspirations when she was writing about me, and had spent many hours just listening over tea when I talked about my challenges, far beyond what she needed to do her job. She was such a dedicated reporter, but beyond that, she was someone who cared deeply about our community and the individuals in it. She showed up to that race to cheer me on, too.

Unfortunately, it was the first race I tried to quit. Three times. The air was heavy that day, and that made it difficult to breathe. I kept having panic attacks, almost from the start of the race, and I would break down in tears, sit down, and decide I couldn't finish. But Sean kept grabbing my hand and coaxing me onward.

"This is just a beautiful day, and we're enjoying the streets of New Haven, full of people," he said.

After setting a post-trauma personal record in a 10K the week before, this was my slowest time ever. But I decided to give myself twenty-four hours to rest and then get back to training again. As one cycling brother said to me, "It's not about coming in first; it's about persevering to the finish."

I was becoming an expert on perseverance.

Before the trauma, I had hoped to do a full marathon and an Ironman by 2013; now it had been pushed back, but completing both remained a goal. I didn't know when my body would be ready, but my mind was already there. When you can imagine something, you can achieve it. It's amazing how much you can influence your own destiny by visualizing yourself succeeding.

By the time my kidney surgery came around, I had named them. My "good" kidney was Bonnie and my "bad" one was Clyde. Clyde had come around somewhat—he was now hovering at about 20 percent functionality, so there was more of a shot at keeping him, but it was still a big question mark. If the surgeon didn't feel he could improve the damage, then it would be more of a liability keeping him in there and waiting for more infections.

"They're a team, you know," I explained to my surgeon the week before surgery. "They really want to stick together. Inside my body."

"And we're going to do our best to make that happen. But we won't know for sure until we get in there."

Sean and I sneaked in one more half marathon right before the surgery date, and we both set personal records. I was glad to have filled up my joy tank, because the medical stuff was never any fun. I had four needle sticks before the phlebotomist gave up and went through my wrist instead. Then there was lots of pre-op testing and paperwork, culminating in my twenty-second surgery in less than two years—and instead of watching the number of surgeries left tick down, somehow I was seeing it go up. I still had at least seven more to come.

"I'm scared," I whispered to Sean through my oxygen mask as I lay on the operating table.

They had allowed him to come into the OR with me until I fell asleep. He stood before me in blue scrubs, a hat, and a surgical mask, and held my hands with his latex-free gloves. "We're going to get through this," he promised.

"Just breathe deep," the anesthesiologist said.

"Please, dear God, let me wake up," I prayed. "Regardless if I keep this kidney or not...let me wake up again. Let me recover. Let me continue to be a wife, a daughter, a friend, and hopefully a mommy someday."

"Okay, Colleen, within two minutes you will be asleep."

I reached up to feel the side of my husband's face covered by the blue mask, and then everything went fuzzy.

Sean wouldn't see me for almost seven more hours, the time I was in surgery. Just like when I was in a coma, I closed my eyes and hours of my life were taken away from me. It was hard not to feel upset by all the time I'd literally lost—gone, without any memories.

This surgery was a complicated procedure with the goal of removing as much scar tissue as possible from my ureter and kidney. I woke up in the recovery room, sick as always from the anesthesia, terrified, and in terrible pain.

As I began to focus, there stood Sean beside my bed.

"You're here, my Colleen. So is Clyde. They took care of the blockages. The surgery was a bit more intensive than they planned, but everything worked out well. Rest, my love. I am here."

Feeling his hand on my heart, I closed my eyes wordlessly and awoke again an hour later to a rhythmic beeping sound.

"How are you, sweetheart?" A nurse held on to my fingers and gazed at me with big brown eyes. "You sure are a strong woman, a light to all of us…"

My eyes closed involuntarily again.

Beep. Beep. Beep.

When I finally awoke for good an hour later, I learned more about the procedure. They'd made several small incisions into my belly to remove the scar tissue and blockages. I had a ten-inch stent placed back in, and this time it was joined by a catheter and tubing sticking out of my body from within my kidney.

God, go to my roots. Make me strong, I prayed.

I imagined my favorite childhood willow tree, with its swaying limbs brushing over my body and its tiny silvery leaves filtering the air, embracing the way my body contoured into its sprawling roots that climbed above and below the ground. I'd had a favorite willow tree as an adult, too, on a country road next to a farm stand en route to one of my favorite hikes. It was tall and graceful, beautiful in every season—but one day I returned to find that it had been cut down.

"The roots were so sprawling that they were just too invasive," someone explained to me.

This is why a willow tree is tattooed on my back.

God, make my roots that strong. Make me a willow tree.

Throughout the night I kept awakening with PTSD flashbacks and pain. Sean was sleeping by my side again, and a nurse who came in for pain management looked over at him and said, "You two have such strength between you."

As much as I had suffered, so had Sean. He had been my rock through every bad day, and my inspiration on the good ones. I never took for granted how lucky I was to have someone like him, and I wished that everyone else who'd been through trauma could have someone just like him, too. He was the reason I fought so hard.

For some reason, I hadn't expected the kidney surgery to be as painful as it was. I'd been through so much already that I was looking at this one more as a routine matter, but even through the narcotics, it was a rough time.

"What did you expect? You had major, major surgery," my surgeon said with a little laugh in his voice. "I had to dissect your midsection even to get to your kidney and ureters. Your kidney was in the wrong place, by the way—it was stuck behind your pancreas, so I had to move it. You still have a lot of scar tissue left; I just took out what I needed to so I could get the job done. I also had to remove a section of your ureter that was too narrowed down to work effectively, and then I removed the lower section of your kidney, fixed it, and reattached it."

So Clyde was a bit of a quilted rag doll now. And according to the surgeon, he would never work fully again...he would always hover around the 20 percent mark. But I guess they decided that 20 percent was better than zero, so he got to stay.

"You will feel better, I promise," the surgeon said. "You just have to stay the course."

When my anxiety spiked, I would sometimes hear a soothing voice in my mind, and it took me a while to realize whose it was: It belonged to Susan, the friend who had showed up and read poetry to me the whole time I was in a coma. I have no memory of her doing so, and yet my soul connected her voice to comfort in times of stress.

The next day I stood before the mirror giving myself a sponge bath. Tears welled in my throat at the sight of my naked body, already so disfigured, now bandaged up in four new places where there would be four new incision scars. I stared at my cane handle and my bandages and I remembered to be thankful again, for the surgical team, the nurses, Sean, my friends and family, and for my own imperfect yet still functional body.

"Thanks for sticking it out, Clyde. You're in the best temple I can give you. I'll take you and Bonnie for a run in the sun someday soon, I promise."

It was supposed to be six weeks of no exercise. I started trying to run again at four weeks.

"I don't even want you walking your dogs for another two weeks," the surgeon said. "Most people would still be lying around on painkillers right now."

"I've done a lot of that in my life. I'm pretty sick of it."

"Nothing more than walking for two more weeks. Got it?"

"Fine."

I had a 5K scheduled the following week. I promised to walk it instead.

Don't tell him I wogged.

Chapter 18

Three Trials

THE YEAR 2014 BROUGHT three very different types of trials into my life, beginning with the case against the freight truck company.

I had been electric with emotion before the first scheduled conference back in 2012, thinking I was about to face in court the man who had run me over. I had all kinds of thoughts bouncing around—wanting to feel compassion, but also knowing that he had not once reached out to apologize or check in on me. On the scene, he had lied to the police and said the crash was my fault. The next day he apologized *to the police* and said that he had seen me, but he couldn't stop in time. As a result, he got an infraction for failure to yield to a pedestrian or cyclist.

That's it.

He almost killed me and he tried to drive away. I ended up with years of surgeries, massive medical costs, a permanently broken body, PTSD, anxiety attacks, an inability to have a baby, an inability to make love with my husband...and he ended up with a ticket. No criminal charges.

We were still living on loans at that point, nervously praying that the settlement would be enough to cover them. The only positive development was Obamacare. Thanks to the Affordable Care Act, my insurance went from $1,800 a month to less than $400, and my deductible was cut in half, too. We would save $1,400 a month in loans.

Before that first meeting, I lost sleep over how I would feel looking into the driver's eyes, wondering what he was going to be like, what I would learn about his background, what he would say to me (if anything). I had tried so many times in my mind to give him the benefit of the doubt; he was scared, he was shocked. I hoped he felt deep remorse not only for his careless driving, but also for trying to flee the scene afterward. I worked to pull myself together and face him.

But he wasn't there.

He wasn't at any of the other conferences, either. I knew that he would eventually have to show up for questioning, but I had no idea of the timetable; my attorney had warned us that a case like this could drag on for two or more years.

Throughout 2014, I had an endless stream of legal paperwork and many angst-filled meetings with my attorneys to prepare, and finally, the depositions began. The first one was of the only witness who had seen the entire thing: David Smith, the construction worker who had been on his lunch break at the deli and was the first to rush to my side. I was not allowed to thank him, hug him, or even speak to him until the trial was over, but I was allowed to be in the room when he was deposed. I hoped that I would manage to convey my gratitude with my eyes.

Listening to him recount every detail he remembered was hard. He described how he wanted to make sure I would live, and that he tried to cover my body with a contractor's tarp because my clothes had been ripped off. It was an honor to be in the same room with him, finally. Sean squeezed my hand as we listened to this man reveal the horrors of what he had seen—and what I had lived. Even though I remembered so much about the trauma, and even though I had told the story hundreds of times by then, there were still details that could take my breath away. I had known my trauma only from my own perspective. It was chilling hearing it from an onlooker's point of view.

There were also fresh new sources of humiliation to come with the trial, such as when a photographer had to come take photos of all my scars and damaged parts...we had to show exactly what permanent effects I had, which meant the photographer would have to see my naked body and take the most intimate pictures for strangers to see and judge. I usually looked forward to photo sessions for magazines and newspapers; not this time.

While the trial was going on, I was trying to book as many speaking gigs as possible. I spoke at schools, races, blood drives, medical conferences, and community events. Bart Yasso of *Runner's World* would introduce me when I spoke at the Gasparilla Distance Classic pre-race event, and then celebrate with me every time I crossed a finish line that weekend (four of them with my brother Erin and his family). It felt so good to be doing something positive for work again. I hadn't felt settled into any kind of career path after the PeaceJam days, but I finally realized that I could make a real difference just by sharing my story.

Of course, public speaking is not an easy way to make a living, and we supplemented it with other things. Sean got trained to teach spin classes, and he started coaching on the weekends. We also sometimes spoke together. Matt Long, who had become a friend by then, told me, "Be patient. Before you know it, your calendar will be full." As with everything else in life, though, I didn't want to be patient. I wanted to be booked in every city, ahead of every race I ran or cycled.

June 2014 brought the next trial, though a different kind. My EMT Amanda, the one who had placed her hand over my heart, received wonderful and devastating news all at once. She and her husband, Chris, who were both firefighters and EMTs who often worked together, found out that they were going to have their first baby. Just a few days later, her legs gave out from under her as she was getting into a fire truck, just as she had done over and over before when answering emergency calls. Chris helped her up the steps, and they later went for a medical evaluation.

Pem McNerney called me in Colorado with the news the day after we finished the Boulder half Ironman.

"It looks like Amanda has ALS," she said. "Lou Gehrig's disease. Her mother and grandmother died of it, too."

I didn't know what to say besides, "Oh my God. I'll ask everyone to pray for her." My heart sank, as my cousin was afflicted with this disease and his muscles had already atrophied. Spencer was a master woodworker and incredibly talented artist. He also had a fearless heart for God and his family.

Amanda was not even thirty years old, and she knew that pregnancy could hasten her decline. ALS is an incurable degenerative disease that ends in death—there's really no way to pretty it up. It's just a matter of how long it takes, and in her case, they learned that she had the most aggressive form of the disease. Doctors would not reassure her that either she or her baby would live; it was unusual for babies to survive to term in this situation.

Amanda had lived her life knowing that she was at risk for this disease, but chose not to go for genetic testing earlier. Instead, she had made the decision to live the healthiest lifestyle she could—which included a vegetarian diet and running—and hope that she was in the 50 percent of children who would not inherit familial ALS.

Within weeks of her diagnosis, she had already lost most of the strength in her legs. I hadn't called right away because I didn't feel I had any right to intrude during such a difficult time. Once a week had passed, though, I wanted to visit and let her know that I would be there for her as much as possible.

The first time I saw her, in early June, she was using a walker. The next time I visited, just a week later, she was in a wheelchair and using an oxygen mask as needed. The following time, she had lost use of her arms and the oxygen mask had to be strapped on. It was shocking to see this vibrant young woman declining so quickly. My cousin Spencer was already bedridden, so I knew the horror of how the disease would progress.

I fought back tears the first time I saw her, and she quickly corrected me. "There's no room for sad energy here with this baby.

We can only have positivity. I want this baby to only know joy and love."

"I'm sorry," I said, biting back my emotion.

"Even though my life is being taken away, God gave me this gift of life and I'm going to protect this peanut no matter what."

"I know you're going to be the best mother."

"And when I pass, my life is going to be used to help solve the puzzle of this disease."

I did what I knew best to do: I signed up for a half marathon as a fundraiser toward Amanda's expenses and asked friends and family to donate. Their small house would have to be modified to open up doorways for her wheelchair to fit through, and she would need a wheelchair van, a Hoyer lift, a commode, and lots of medical equipment. Their medical bills were already soaring, but would eventually be outrageous. This couple who had been there for their community in so many ways now needed as much support as we could give.

"Thank you for putting your hand over *my* heart now," Amanda wrote on my Facebook page.

I ran those 13.1 miles questioning myself and God, asking why I was saved from the brink of death while Amanda had a terminal disease. I prayed for total healing; I prayed for a miracle for both her and my cousin. My own healing had been a miracle, so why not two more? How does He decide who gets a miracle and who doesn't? Why did I have so much guilt for surviving?

The community responded to Amanda's need in an astounding way: After many fundraisers across the shoreline—everything from dinners to auctions to dance classes, bake sales, and car washes—the

GoFundMe total reached over $350,000, enough to build Amanda and Chris an entirely new, accessible modular house with all the equipment they needed. Not only that, but contractors volunteered their time and businesses donated needed supplies.

After developing a high fever, I was treated for severe cellulitis (a bacterial skin infection) at Yale on July 24 and released with a prescription for antibiotics six times a day. It was a problem I would have to face for the rest of my life, but it was treatable. Amanda was admitted into the hospital two days later for the rest of her pregnancy so doctors could monitor her oxygen and protect the baby; her breathing was so labored that they had to perform a tracheotomy. After that, she couldn't speak at all, and never would again. She learned to communicate using her eyes on a screen that would translate her letters into robotically spoken words in a female voice.

No matter what, she never lost her sense of humor and I never saw her cry. She had a cartoon photograph of Ursula from *The Little Mermaid* on her breathing machine, so she called it Ursula. Her unborn child—who they soon learned would be a girl—was nicknamed Peanut. Amanda talked very openly about the realities of her disease, but held out hope that she would be around to meet her baby and see her grow up for as long as possible. Of course, we all prayed for a cure to be discovered in time.

In August, the Bridgeport Bluefish baseball team did a big fundraiser for Amanda and Chris, and they invited me to throw the first pitch in her honor. I had never thrown a softball properly before, and I said to Amanda, "I don't want to screw this up for you!"

Sean helped teach me how to throw a decent pitch over the next couple of weeks, and I got out there and did it, writing *For Little Peanut* on the ball in Sharpie and saving it for her afterward, figuring I would put it in a glass display case.

"She's going to really appreciate that when she gets older," Amanda told me.

Sean and I often went to visit Amanda together in the beginning, and we'd bring essential oils and massage her feet and hands, which were so stiff. She lost abilities one by one—a few fingers could still move for a while, but then they stopped. By the end, she was completely paralyzed.

She defied all expectations, though. She became one of the rare ALS patients to carry a baby to full term. Arabella was healthy and beautiful, and Amanda got to meet her baby and take her home. Amanda needed twenty-four-hour medical care, but she was able to be home with her husband and daughter instead of in a hospital. Not only that, but she survived for a year and a half beyond that point to see her little girl growing and developing a personality. During that time, Spencer passed away in his sleep, and our family mourned. It was terrible to know that this disease would claim both of them in such a short time span.

When I went to visit Amanda, I got to hold this beautiful baby—and ache for how unfair it all was. It hurt to know that Arabella would never hear her mother's voice, or experience what an active and vibrant person Amanda had been. It hurt to think of such joy being mixed with such tragedy. I tried hard to respect Amanda's wishes, though, and stay positive.

Let there be no room in my heart for sadness here, I prayed. *Just fill me with love.*

"I want you to meet a friend of mine, Karen," Amanda told me one day. "You would love her—she's crazy like you. She does Ironman events. She never stops."

I did get to meet Karen at a triathlon in 2015. It was my first triathlon after another surgery, and I was in so much pain that I was puking on the side of the road...and that's when Karen came bounding over to me, asking, "Are you Colleen?"

Mortifying. Yet she still decided to be my friend.

We agreed to do an ALS ride together for Amanda and Spencer, which happened so soon after Karen had given birth to a surrogate baby that she had to stop and pump her breasts all throughout the ride—and the mother would meet us to pick up the pumped milk along the trail! When we crossed the finish line together, we FaceTimed Amanda to celebrate with her. I wished I could FaceTime Spencer also, but I took comfort through the tears knowing he was no longer suffering, free from this disease and hopefully creating beautiful artwork in heaven.

As time went on, though, it became harder and harder for me to visit Amanda. I would hold on to her limp hand and pray that God would *do something* and allow her to squeeze back. I was on the verge of breaking down every time, and usually did in the car afterward. It was so emotionally draining that, I'm embarrassed to say, I began avoiding it. My plan was to visit her weekly, but I became too fearful to do it because I didn't think I could hold it together the way she wanted me to. It was clear that she didn't have much time left, but no one knew how she would go. Amanda had helped to save my life, and now I was powerless to do the same for her.

I never questioned God as much as I did during those times. *Why* would *You* do this? Why would *You* take away my ability to have a baby, and then allow Amanda to find out she was dying at the same time she found out she was having a baby? What kind of plan is this?

Spencer had been much older when he was diagnosed, and he'd had children and a beautiful, long life. ALS is ugly no matter the age of affliction, but this young? I wished I didn't know what was ahead for her.

My days were so mixed with good and bad at that time. The final trial in 2014 was my own medical one: It was time at last for me to start the process of skin expanders so that my thin, tight skin could be removed and "good" skin could be sewn on in its place, to reduce the risk of infection and cancer and to allow me more freedom of movement. What that meant was that a surgeon would make incisions and place silicone balloons underneath the healthy areas of my skin in three places on my leg and hip, then fill the bags with saline slowly over the course of several months so that my skin would grow to accommodate it—like when skin stretches and grows during a pregnancy.

The initial surgery would take three hours, then the expansion process would span about four months. During that time, I was advised, there could be "some discomfort" as the skin stretched. At the end, there would be a second surgery to remove the expanders, cut away the fragile "bad" skin, and reposition the healthy tissue over those areas.

I decided to try accomplishing one big goal before going for the initial surgery: I wanted to try running a full marathon.

Without telling people, I signed up for the Via Marathon sponsored by the Lehigh Valley Health Network. To my amazement, none other than Bart Yasso himself offered to let Sean and me stay at his house that weekend. How could I turn that down? I felt like I was in the presence of a legend, and it was so good to see up close just how much Bart cared about runners and running. When I realized, much to my chagrin, that I hadn't packed socks, Bart rummaged through his drawers to find a pair that would fit me. They must have been lucky socks, because I finished that marathon.

I came in nearly dead last, and I had pain, bathroom issues, and tears along the way, but I finished—all 26.2 miles, as Sean situated himself along the route to cheer and scream for me every four to six miles. I couldn't stop crying afterward.

Then I turned myself over to my doctors.

Amanda was in the hospital being monitored a few floors below me when the three expanders were implanted into my body. There were complications from the surgery (I had a lot of blood loss and a major hematoma on my hip), but I was discharged two days later with strict instructions not to walk or put any weight on my legs for the next several months, with exceptions for going to the bathroom or other brief movements in the house using a walker. I was to use a wheelchair at all times outside the house. I would come back to Yale weekly at first, and then twice a week, to fill the expanders with saline in the three ports.

My dogs were also not allowed to jump on me or cuddle me in bed, which was so confusing for them and sad for me. I asked my friends to please come walk the dogs for me, since I wasn't allowed to anymore and Sean worked during the day. People were again willing to come watch over me and bring me meals, but I just needed to be solo for a while; I was in pain and made bad company. I knew the surgery was an important step, though, so I kept my head high about it.

I also had permission to work my upper body and lightly exercise my right leg from a seated position, so I got straight on that. Lucky me that I had a perfect place nearby for rehab and strength training: The local gym had great equipment and great trainers.

As soon as I could, I got back on a bike—a handcycle one. I also signed up for my first "wheelchair 5K." But before I could get there, I had another ER visit: After wound care at Yale, I bled so much that I awoke in bed at home with pools of blood all over the sheets. That triggered my PTSD and the panic attacks were unrelenting.

Sean took me to the hospital, where they told me it was "old blood" from a surgical hematoma, and that as long as it was brown, I needed to let it keep coming out. For sixteen hours I watched cups and cups of blood pour out of my leg until it finally slowed down. They gave me IV fluids and antibiotics and sent me home, where we would continue to do wound care six times a day.

Just a few days after that, I was scheduled to give the keynote speech at a Women in Cable Telecommunications event called Propel Yourself: Overcoming Challenges to Propel You to a Better Future. I gave my speech from a chair, and at the end of it, during the Q&A session that always followed, I noticed that my leg was bleeding through my bandages. Luckily, they had placed a towel under me for just this scenario, so I managed not to ruin the Marriott Hotel chair. Sean and my friend and coordinator Michelle Peters whisked me into my wheelchair and off into a room for a quick wound dressing change, and then I was back in a flash to continue talking to the people and thanking them for coming.

Luckily, I was still able to do my next marathon in Rhode Island on a low-to-the-ground hand-crank bike borrowed from Gaylord—one of the bikes they bought with the money from the cycling tour fundraiser. Hand-crank bikes allow riders to keep their legs straight, safe, and buckled in. It was exhilarating to find out what it felt like to lead the pack in a run! For seven miles, I was out front by myself before the elite athletes caught up to me. Then it was a game: I'd get ahead of them on downhills, then they'd zip past me on inclines. Little did I know I got a flat tire about halfway through the race.

It was humbling to watch the perfect form, consistent stride rate, and strength of these phenomenal athletes from my ground-level vantage point. Using my arms to pedal for three hours was super challenging, but it was also a great honor to be able to do it. I knew how sore I was going to be the next day, but the good kind of sore. The kind of sore that reminded me I was still alive and still moving.

I had found by then that every new setback I faced made me stronger in the end, even when it was hard to see it at the time. Fighting for my life made me appreciate my life more. Fighting for mobility meant I'd never take my body for granted again. Fighting off infections and anxiety and PTSD and pain all meant that I was strong enough to handle all of it and still had a purpose.

I was a change maker. Not only was I a product of heroes, but I was becoming one of my own heroes, too. That's what I hoped to convey at all of my talks: We *all* have that power. We are *all* change makers.

Being in a wheelchair was no fun, but I enjoyed the effect it had on other people. When I got up in front of an audience with my leg still wrapped up like a mummy, and told them I had just hand-cycled a marathon, I could see the excuses in their minds fade away. *I'm out of shape. I've never been athletic. I have a bad knee. I don't have time.*

Life is precious!

If you're alive, there's a purpose. Find a way.

My body slowed me down during the expansion process. I just couldn't seem to stop bleeding, and the doctors eventually told me that every time my blood pressure was raised, it was causing blood loss. I had to stop long hand-cycling and wheelchair sessions and limit myself to just chair yoga and strict upper body training for a while. Eventually, once the bleeding stopped, the restrictions were lifted a bit. But by then, the pain was bad enough that even I wasn't ready to push it. It felt like I was being ripped from the inside out. I learned the beauty of naps and sweatpants, and the only marathoning I did was binge-watching television. After each expansion, I would go home in so much pain that I would take Valium and sleep for hours. My muscles would twitch as the skin stretched and burned.

A little girl was getting expanders filled in her forehead at the same time I was getting mine done, and I'd often hear her screaming in pain a couple of rooms away as they did her fills. It was bad enough for me, but I couldn't imagine how confusing it must have been for a child.

This is temporary, I reminded myself. *At the end of this, I'll get to keep my leg, and it'll be better than before. What amazing things our bodies can do!*

And no matter what life threw our way, we always had the best people around us to step up and help us get through it. After an angry neighbor complained about the weeds on our property, our friends showed up to help Sean with the yardwork while I stayed in bed. A not-angry neighbor scheduled a cleaning service to come in toward the end of my treatments so I wouldn't have to bend over to clean the floors.

The expanders caused me to look bulbous and deformed as they were filled; the one on my thigh looked suspiciously like I was concealing a football under it, so I drew a football on my skin to make the surgeon laugh. My butt, on the other hand—I have never had such a badonkadonk in my life! The hip expander made it so enormous on one side that Sean and I found it endlessly entertaining. I was shakin' my groove thang and "Baby Got Back"-ing it all over the place. It caused some practical issues, though: I could no longer fit in my wheelchair, or in my normal clothes.

I decided my three new additions needed names, so my quad expander became Buffy, my hip/butt expander became Swank (like Hilary Swank, because I've always had a girl crush on her), and my inner thigh expander was Marcel, like Marcel the Shell.

They got kicked out on January 2, 2015, in a six-hour surgery. When I awoke, I had two wound drains in, and a lot of pain medication that didn't solve my pain. It was awful. I had developed a severe allergic reaction to morphine due to the excessive amounts given to me during the initial trauma and many surgeries that followed, so that go-to painkiller was off the table and I had to use less-effective ones.

Thanks to my insurance, though, I was kicked out of the hospital after just one night. I could barely move, I was in enormous pain, and no one thought I was ready to go. But that's modern-day insurance for you.

At home, I would have Sean and my home health care nurse. I was confined to bed rest for the first few days, except for standing to use a modified urinal. Slowly—way too slowly, it felt—I improved, and found ways to make myself useful. Gail came over for a sewing session so we could make some pretty hospital gowns for Amanda (it was completely driving me crazy that she was lying there in standard-issue gowns made by the company whose driver ran me over). When we were able, Sean and I visited my family in Pennsylvania.

After not being able to run for more than seven months, I got a little stir-crazy. I would watch the runners run past my house in the mornings and cheer them on. One day I brought out a cowbell. Every time a runner went past, I would bang on that cowbell and yell out in encouragement. It was usually well received, if unexpected. Who doesn't need more cowbell in their lives?

It was good for me, too. Being out there on the roads was great, but being someone's support felt right, too. I thought about all the people who had encouraged me along the way, both dear friends and strangers whose faces blurred together along a race path, and I thought of how much love there was in the world. Sometimes it's hard to see. Sometimes it's obscured by mountains of crap. But it's there, and I was ready to amplify it. Love always wins.

Chapter 19

Endings and Beginnings

THE FIRST TIME I came face-to-face with the man who ran me over was at his deposition in 2015. He was a Hispanic man who communicated with the court through a translator. Sean and I sat across the table from him and his attorney. He looked like a sad man. He seemed rather old, not only physically but in spirit.

My feelings of anger were mixed with questions about where he came from, why he'd left his home country, what his family was like, and mostly, what in his spirit made him look me in the eyes and run me over and then try to continue driving onward? I wanted to understand how a fellow human detaches from another human in this way. As I listened to him answer the questions, and then heard his answers translated from Spanish to English, many times I squeezed Sean's hand and tried not to grimace.

"Did you feel your truck go up and down as it rolled over her body?"

"Yes, like I went over two bumps."

"Did you hear her screaming?"

"No."

I could not stop staring at him, reading every tattoo on his arms, the lines on his face, and the hairs on his head. This was my brother, yet we were worlds apart.

When he was asked to recount that day, he did so with agony, asking, "Why am I being forced to relive such a day that's caused me so many nightmares?"

I was furious. *He* had nightmares? I thought of all the letters I never sent begging him to find human compassion, begging him to acknowledge just a tiny fraction of my pain and sorrow for my body and my womb that was filled only with scar tissue. Toward the end of his questioning, I was so overcome with emotion and flashbacks that my heart raced and I feared I would pass out.

He finally said, "Please, no more questions. I can't bear to recount any more of this."

I had finally had it. I'd sat there so perfectly quietly, wearing a sundress that was soft upon my injured skin. I stood up and said, "You want to know what it feels like to experience panic and remember every day what the horror feels and looks like? LOOK AT ME!"

I lifted my dress to expose my scarred body. My attorney, very cool and collected, said, "Colleen, okay, he gets it. Put your dress down."

If I'd had the opportunity, I would have stripped off my underwear and sat on the table in front of him and made them translate,

"THIS IS WHAT IT LOOKS LIKE WHEN SOMEONE'S LABIA ARE RIPPED OFF, and see this? THIS IS WHAT IT LOOKS LIKE WHEN SOMEONE'S ASS IS GUTTED FROM INSIDE OUT." I wanted to show him everything. I wanted him to touch the tire tracks on my abdomen. I wanted him to feel for a minute a fraction of the burning pain I felt. I wanted him to understand the agony of not being able to make love to your spouse for years because everything was pulled off, then stapled and put back on, and crooked, and nerve damaged, and full of immense pain. I wanted him to feel what it was like not to have control over your sphincters, to let out loud farts all the damn time at humiliating moments and not be able to stop it. I wanted him to know what it feels like to sneeze and urinate on yourself because you've been catheterized so long and have so much damage. I wanted him to feel his cartilage crackle when he rolled over while sleeping in bed and know it's because his sternum is disconnected. I wanted him to feel what it was like to be trapped in a comatose body with a breathing machine, a feeding tube, and nurses rolling him over all day long to keep him from having bedsores. There was *so much* I wanted to say and do, but I simply put my dress back down and sobbed.

Sean wrapped his arms around me and walked me out of the office.

A few months later, we had a private settlement offer. In a flash, it was over. The price of all I had suffered and would suffer, all we had lost, was set on a piece of paper. It was never a human process, just a monetary figure. The legal system is adept at dehumanizing the process, with its lineup of suits and clipboards and pens clicking away.

We could have pursued the matter further in trial, but it had eaten us up enough. We had millions of dollars in medical bills and loans to pay back, and we just wanted it all to be over, so we accepted the offer.

I called my chief trauma surgeon that night to tell him it was finished.

"Now what?" I asked him. "I don't know where we go from here. How do I make a positive impact on the world from such a negative situation?"

Dr. Kaplan said, "You lived, warrior. You are alive. The case is settled. No matter your compensation amount, you're untethered. You know what you need to do. Your passions and will have not changed. Continue the course without this hanging over you any longer. Hug your husband, get away for a while, and embrace that you are here."

I liked what he said. Untethered. I was finally allowed to speak to David Smith, the contractor who had run out to save my life. I was able to settle the debts and exhale. As unfair as it all felt to put a dollar figure on what we'd lost, and as unsatisfying as it was never to get a real apology from the driver, it was time to move on to our next chapter.

That meant surrounding ourselves with things that water our souls, fertilize our roots, and help us grow. Sean and I became active board members for Bike Walk Connecticut, which meant that we would lead the charge on cyclist and pedestrian safety in our state. I continued my work as a board member and volunteer spokesperson for the American Red Cross. We began working to have Jamis and Coda certified as emotional support dogs so they could help us do good work with the Red Cross. I continued to expand my horizons as a motivational speaker and encourage people to donate blood and learn CPR. We grew bigger gardens. We got our friends up and moving. We showed up at blood drives. We promised never to forget or squander the second chances we both were given.

Although I wanted to go, go, go, my goal for getting myself back to training kept getting pushed back. I had a large mass on my left leg that wouldn't shrink, so doctors had to insert a drain and break up multiple blood clots. My PTSD went into overdrive watching all the blood pour out of my leg; it felt like I was watching myself bleed out on the pavement all over again.

I slowly worked my way up to being active again, starting with walking, indoor cycling, swimming, and then a hike in the woods. Finally, by June 2015, I was back to doing triathlons with Sean and collecting medals for my heroes. My body was working again, and that was a major blessing, but there were still physical limitations that would never go away, along with a couple more ER trips when my body became septic. The surgeon was right: Warm public pools and lakes in the midst of summer really were a nightmare for me.

I had to come to a realistic conclusion: The full Ironman that Sean and I had hoped to do together just wasn't going to happen for me.

I watched my husband become a better and better athlete, coming in first out of seventy-five people on the swim portion of a half Ironman that June. This wonderful man had been hanging in there waiting for me because we had done nearly all of our races side by side (or at least with him up front and me bringing up the rear!). This time, I had to let him know that it was okay to go on without me.

Sean loves so much and asks for so little. That November, we flew out to Florida so that he could compete in his first full Ironman race in Panama City. What's amazing is that a neighbor from Connecticut flew out, too, so that she could see her "godson" become an Ironman. Sometimes family has nothing to do with biological relationships.

Sean completed his first full Ironman race November 7, 2015, and I got to be the proudest wife ever.

Amanda couldn't wait to congratulate him, too.

"Keep doing all the glorious things your body can do," she said. It was a sad reminder of all the variations between ability and disability. I had felt so sorry for myself for what I couldn't do, and there was Amanda, refusing to fall into despair even as her entire body was paralyzed and she knew she had reached the end.

Her spirit was so strong, and I was in awe of her attitude. She stayed lucid and encouraging and active online until just days before she died, on September 21, 2016. Her body was transported to a research hospital where they would remove her central nervous system to study, according to her wishes.

The day after her death, I flipped open my Bible, hoping for an answer. This was the passage it landed on:

> Don't fret or worry. Instead of worrying, pray.
> Let petitions and praises shape your worries
> into prayers, letting God know your concerns.
> Before you know it, a sense of God's wholeness,

everything coming together for good, will come and settle you down. It's wonderful what happens when Christ displaces worry at the center of your life.

—Philippians 4:6–7

As I continued to look for ways to quiet my own worries and focus outward rather than inward, I was delighted to hear from a woman named Barbara who had originally met me at the Superhero Half Marathon I did with my walker, and then heard me give a keynote speech at the Wineglass Marathon. She emailed to ask if I would be her guide at the Redding Road Race Half Marathon in the spring of 2017.

"I understand you have physical and mental limitations, but so do I," she wrote. "You've become a role model to me and it would mean so much to have you be my guide and do the journey with me."

I wrote back through tears to accept. The weekend of the race, I put on the yellow Achilles T-shirt once again, except this time it said GUIDE. Sean and I would both serve as guides in races later that month. It's wonderful to be able to give back through an organization that has been there for me.

Throughout this journey, what I've learned more than anything is that we all have an expiration date on our lives, and we will all have big challenges to deal with along the way. But we also have choices in how we approach those challenges, and people who will show up for us in a big way if we let them in. We can wallow alone in our grief, or lose ourselves in anger, or we can choose to love harder and let our love for life and people grow larger than our pain.

I've never been a fan of the phrase "When life hands you lemons, make lemonade," because it always felt wasteful to me. Just lemonade? What about the seeds?

I hope that, through my trauma, I manage to plant seeds in fertile ground—enough for whole lemon groves to pop up all around the world. I may never know exactly what God's plan is for my life, but I know that as long as I'm breathing, I'm going to do my best to live with purpose and gratitude for every moment I get. I will use this once broken, scarred body to spread the most beautiful message I can: Love is always louder.

Acknowledgments

God—By the grace of God, go I. I know my number will eventually be up one of these days. Thank You for giving me the opportunity to be a change maker on this Earth a little while longer. In the face of trauma and grief, it is easy to question Your will and wonder why we face such pain and suffering. I found myself diving deep into prayer seeking guidance and direction. I am grateful for every breath I take. Thank You for showing me Your love through so many that have loved me. Thank You for grace.

Sean Alexander—You showed me kindness and have exemplified love and respect since we dated in high school. Your patience throughout this process has been exceptional. Thank you for engulfing me every day in love and strength. Thank you for believing in me when no one knew if I would breathe on my own. Thank you for supporting me from the moment I woke up through each surgery, each race, and every harebrained idea. Thank you for your willingness to help me live my life to the fullest. Thank you for being my best friend, and my lover even when the physical act of intimacy was destroyed. Thank you for showing me what faithfulness and love should be. Thank you for believing in our story. Thank you for reminding me that it is we. Thank you for holding my hand when doubt filled my soul, and reminding me to pray. Thank you for being a man who is centered in Christ's love. We are truly so much stronger together. I love you.

My family—Thank you for being at my side. You have shown me the never-ending bond of family. My mother and father, you encouraged and watched when I learned to walk for the second time. Thank you for helping me when I learned to eat solid food again, and even when I needed to learn that, despite being completely vulnerable and feeling like a helpless infant, I was still very much a strong woman of value and beauty, and a child of God.

My medical team—To my chief trauma surgeon, Dr. Kaplan, I give eternal gratitude. You are a man I have learned to respect so much over the years. Thank you for your dedication to trauma medicine. Thank you for the integrity, dedication, sweat, and fight you dedicate to every one of your patients. I am so grateful you were there that day. You have become a part of my soul. You were more than my trauma surgeon; you were my "quarterback" who looked over all surgeries and care for the next several years. You chose to allow yourself to be available for my many emails and questions. Your professionalism never wavered and yet you allowed yourself to also be available for psychological needs, as I had many. Thank you for always being honest with me. You are a fierce and loyal wolf in the field of medicine. Thank you.

To my orthopedic surgeon and fellow cyclist Dr. Baumgaertner, thank you for screwing me back together. Thank you for treating me like the wife, daughter, sister, friend, and cyclist that I am, and not simply a patient. Thank you for helping me bike and run again.

Dr. Persing, thank you for saving my leg. Thank you for your patience through years of surgeries and expansion. Thank you for believing in me.

Dr. Reddy, thank you for helping to piece me back together while treating me with such respect and dignity.

To the rest of my surgeons, I say thank you. Thank you for letting me hug you pre- and post-op, thank you for putting the human element strongly back into the OR pre- and post-. To my SICU nurses, I do not remember many of your faces from the time I spent in the coma; however, I remember your voices and the care and integrity you provided to me while I could not provide for myself.

To the staff at Gaylord, you all believed in me and never sugarcoated the state I was in, or what still lay ahead of me and the potential complications. I would not have recovered and been able to continue to heal and thrive without you. To my home healthcare professionals, I love you all. To my physical therapists, massage therapists, occupational therapists, emotional therapist Leslie Hyman, thank you. To the Madison EMS, firefighters, and police, you guys are our front line. Thank you for being everyday heroes.

Friends—You went above and beyond helping to take care of me after the trauma. You were also strong forces of encouragement as I began writing this memoir. Thank you eternally. I know at times it was quite trying and even a bit awkward. Your laughter, tears, hugs, shower help while holding tubes, gross wound care, and sarcasm are forever appreciated.

Mentors—Thank you, Matt Long, for being available to talk and be a mentor throughout my journey. Thank you for being a role model and showing me what I can achieve. Thank you for sharing your story of survival with the world to help others know they can say, "I will." Thank you, Jody Williams, for being a force of nature. Thank you for teaching me and thousands of others across the globe that "emotion without action is irrelevant." Thank you for showing me that I can rise and be an advocate for change. Thank you, Bart Yasso, for being so open, and full of love and support. Thank you for being the ambassador of the running community. Thank you for helping me understand my value as a runner, even though I felt broken, slow, and unworthy.

My literary team—To my agent, Sorche Fairbank; and my beautiful, patient, and amazingly talented ghostwriter, Jenna Glatzer; my editor Christina Boys; Hannah Phillips; Laura Cherkas; and Center Street Publishing: What an honor to work with such a committed and talented team. Thank you to Scott Rigsby for introducing me to Jenna.

Blood donors—You selflessly give your time and your blood. You are heroes. Thank you for giving me the gift of life.

Bill Bloss—You are a humble and selfless man. You were an incredible rock for us and a fierce protector as we went forward through years of pain, fear, anger, and frustration. Thank you for treating us as a human family and for respecting us. You are an incredible man of so much integrity, and we have been honored by you.

How to Be a Hero

My life would have ended in 2011 were it not for the heroes who showed up. There are so many ways to be somebody's future hero; here are a few of the ways that resonate with me.

1. Donate blood.

Every two seconds, someone in the United States needs blood—which includes trauma patients, those being treated for cancer, people with sickle-cell disease, those with complications from surgery, and many others. The average red blood cell transfusion is three pints. I needed seventy-eight units just in the first seventy-two hours! This included *platelets* (which help blood coagulate and are essential for trauma patients), *plasma* (needed by burn, trauma, and cancer patients), and *whole blood*.

There is a critical need for platelets because they cannot be stored for more than five days and are always in demand. To donate platelets, you must be at least sixteen years old (seventeen in some states). It's a longer process that must be done at a Red Cross center (not at a blood drive), and you can donate up to twenty-four times a year. Six whole blood donations must be separated and pooled to provide a single platelet transfusion. However, one apheresis platelet donation provides enough platelets for one complete transfusion.

To donate plasma, you must have type AB blood, which is very rare (only 4 percent of donors). It takes a little over an hour and can only be done at select Red Cross donation centers.

For more information visit www.redcrossblood.org.

2. Learn CPR and first aid.

CPR does work! You can register for CPR and first aid classes through most town halls, get information from your local libraries, or visit www.redcross.org to find classes near you. The Red Cross offers classes across the globe. You never know when you'll encounter an emergency situation—would you know how to effectively and safely perform CPR on a child, do the Heimlich maneuver, or help someone who's fainted in front of you? Take the class and refresh your knowledge every couple of years.

3. Learn the "Rules of the Road" for cycling and pedestrian safety.

Educate yourself as a motorist, pedestrian, and cyclist. It is everyone's responsibility to be safe and respectful to one another on our streets. Bicyclists have the same rights and responsibilities on the road as drivers, so pass safely and don't squeeze cyclists off the road. Model safe driving and riding to younger individuals. Pledge not to text and drive, and use patience behind the wheel.

Remember, we are role models and examples, and everyone is someone's everything!

For cyclists, visit www.bikeleague.org/content/rules-road-0 for bike rules and videos, and remember that helmets save lives! For fun and functional helmets for all ages, check out www. nutcasehelmets.com.

4. Support the ALS Foundation.
I made a promise to Amanda and her daughter as well as my cousin Spencer that I would continue spreading the message of the need for funds to help find a cure for ALS. Visit www.als.org.

5. Support your local fire/EMS station.
Most firefighters and emergency medical workers help on a volunteer or per diem basis and rely heavily on private donations to offset the many costs of running an emergency management service. Visit your fire department and ask how you can help. Aside from financial donations, they might also need help with things like mailings, writing letters, or planning events.

6. Be a mentor.
Look for local programs that can connect you with at-risk kids who could really use support and guidance. You can find them through Big Brothers Big Sisters of America, youth centers, crisis centers, and school social workers. You don't need to be a teacher, a parent, or a perfect person—you just need to be willing to invest some time with a young person who may not have good role models.

7. Become a guide for a challenged athlete or volunteer to help with events.

Achilles International asks for volunteers to run or walk with disabled athletes both during training and during events. You can sign up here: www.achillesinternational.org/volunteers. You can also get involved with other organizations that benefit challenged athletes, such as Dare2Tri (www.dare2tri.org), the Scott Rigsby Foundation (www.scottrigsbyfoundation.org), the Challenged Athletes Foundation (www.challengedathletes.org), and Special Olympics (www.specialolympics.org). You don't need athletic ability to help out with things like handing out water, helping at the sign-in station, helping athletes with transitions during triathlons, or fundraising for equipment and race sponsorships. It is so empowering for disabled athletes to retain their identity; do what you can to be a part of that.

8. Be a force for peace.

In this increasingly tumultuous time, find ways to chip in to solve local and global problems. For more information on PeaceJam, go to www.peacejam.org. You can also help out in the organization's quest to achieve one billion acts of peace at www.billionacts.org. There, you can create your own act of peace or join in on someone else's.

9. Express your gratitude.

You never know when someone really needs to hear your words or have you show your appreciation of the kindness they show others. I found a tangible way to express my gratitude by giving away my medals. What can you do to show people that they make a difference?

10. HONOR YOURSELF!

Learn to be gentle to yourself and remember to love yourself. Treat yourself like you would treat any young person; that same young version of you is still part of your soul. Be your own hero! Remember, if we do not provide our own self-care and self-love, we cannot be strong for others. Take time in your life to pray, and find gratitude in even the littlest things.

About the Authors

Colleen Kelly Alexander (www.colleenkellyalexander.com) is a life-long athlete and motivational speaker. With her indomitable spirit and amazing story of survival, Colleen teaches others how to aim higher, be stronger, and use adversity as a catalyst to make themselves and the world better. She was the executive director of the Common Ground Youth Center in Vermont for eight years and a regional program manager for PeaceJam, where Nobel Peace laureates mentor youth. She has also worked for, volunteered for, and is heavily involved with the Red Cross. She lives in a New England coastal town with her husband and their three dogs and cat.

Jenna Glatzer (www.jennaglatzer.com) is the author or ghostwriter of twenty-nine books, including Celine Dion's authorized biography and *The Marilyn Monroe Treasures*. She and her daughter live in New York.